My Planner

for Study & Other Cool Stuff

Targeting Executive Functioning skills for Teens:

- Goal Setting
- Planning
- Organization
- Time Management
- Self-Management
- and more

Developed by: Stephanie Chan, Ph.D.c., M.Ed., BCBA

My Name: ______________________

School: ______________________

Grade: ______________________

First published in 2023 by
Society for Behavior SciAnts, BC, V5H 1K6, Canada

Publisher's Note
This publication is designed to provide accurate and authoritative information about the subject matter. If expert assistance or therapy is needed, the services of a competent professional should be sought.

Table of Contents

Introduction

Some Common Academic Challenges That Middle and High School Students Face

Middle and high school students are at the stage of building good work habits for future higher education and jobs. However, you may feel overwhelmed by schoolwork and need help figuring out where to start. You may have challenges balancing study and play, planning homework, managing time to complete it, and submitting it on time. You may have difficulty focusing on work. Yet, you may often forget to take homework home or to school. You may be very talented and hardworking, but you still face some of the above challenges hampering you from academic success.

If this is the case, you are not alone.

How Are These Challenges Related to Executive Functioning Skills and the Corresponding Behaviors?

Studies have indicated that academic performance in school is related to executive functions (Sesma et al., 2009; Zelazo & Carlson, 2012), including working memory, impulse control, problem-solving, and planning (Pascual, et al., 2019). From the perspective of behavior analysis, the components of executive functioning skills needed to achieve academic success and conquer the abovementioned challenges can be broken down into the following behaviors:

Short-Term Memory

- Able to attend to auditory and visual information in group and individual settings
- Able to recall past events and related information
- Able to attend to current or important tasks and stay focused

Continued on next page

Introduction, Cont.

Imagine if a student has challenges with the above skills, they may miss information in the class and not be able to recall what has been taught and what homework needs to be done. As a result, they may forget to bring homework home.

Impulse Control

 Able to analyze and choose what is important

 Able to ignore distractions

 Able to self-evaluate, self-regulate, and self-manage

Imagine a student has challenges with the above skills. Homework can be so overwhelming that it becomes a massive, undoable task with which they do not know where to start, and they feel it is impossible to start. As a result, they may choose an easy task (e.g., watching videos on their phone) and delay the homework. Even if they start working, they may be easily distracted and unable to focus on their work.

Problem-Solving

 Able to come up with different ways to solve problems

 Able to flexibly modify the actions when situations change

Imagine if a student has challenges with the above skills, they may keep their original plan even if they are aware that a project is due or a test is coming soon. They may fixate on doing things in a certain way no matter how rushed the homework needs to be finished. As a result, they may often miss deadlines or do poorly on homework and tests.

Continued on next page

Introduction, Cont.

 **Planning**

 Able to set goals

 Able to analyze the different ways to achieve goals and choose the most suitable one

 Able to develop an action plan following a timeline

Imagine if a student has challenges with the above skills, they may start working on homework or preparing for tests at the last minute, which will also make them miss deadlines or do poorly on homework and tests. When they are working on group projects, it will affect the whole group.

If you have any of the above challenges, you are not alone and this planner is for you!

Why This Planner?

This planner utilizes behavior science technology to target the above crucial skills and provide an effective system for middle-school and high-school students who require support in the executive functioning area. This helps in establishing good work habits that may benefit future college study and even lifetime.

To target the short-term memory challenge, the planner offers visual prompts for you to take notes on homework in each class; it also includes a checklist at the end of each school day to remind you to take required items home and a checkbox at the end of the day to remind you to pack all required items in backpack for school next day.

To target the planning challenge, the planner includes step-by-step instructions to help you set goals, plan backward, and allocate time (time management) to complete homework by a deadline.

To address the problem-solving challenge, the section "Situations for Problem-Solving" presents a variety of situations to guide you on how to seek assistance when stuck in class or after school. For example, it includes such social problems as "What if I forget what to do for homework?", "What if I don't know how to solve a problem (in my homework)?", "What if I can't finish it on time?", and so on.

To target the impulse control challenge, the section "Strategies for Staying Focused" provides self-management strategies for you to identify distractors, arrange environment to reduce those distractors, maintain focus, and reward on-task behavior.

How to Use This Planner?

This planner has been designed for middle and high school students to improve executive functioning skills with the guidance and supervision of parents or instructors. To use the planner effectively, please follow the eight steps below.

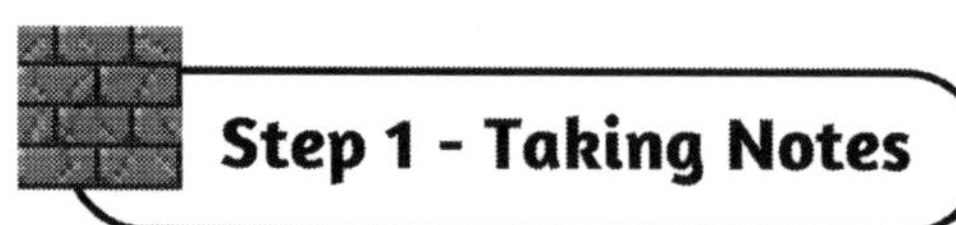

Step 1 - Taking Notes

When you begin using this planner, find the Daily Planner for the current day of the week (e.g. Monday) and record today's date, as illustrated in the example below.

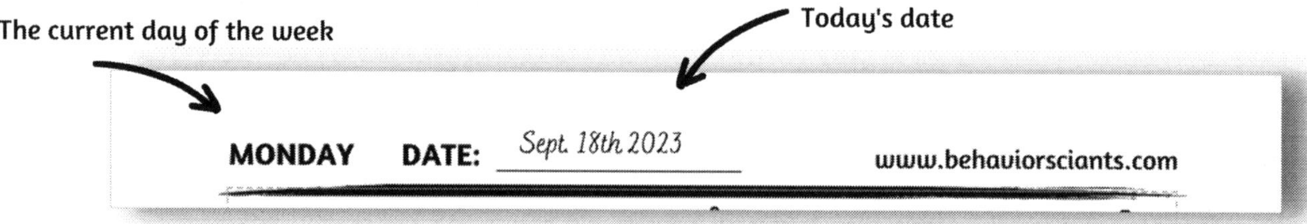

At school, at the end of each class, write down any homework or to-do tasks in the corresponding box on the "HOMEWORK FROM SCHOOL" table, along with their due dates. At the end of the school day, ensure that all homework and tasks are in your backpack and check off the corresponding boxes on the table. See the example below.

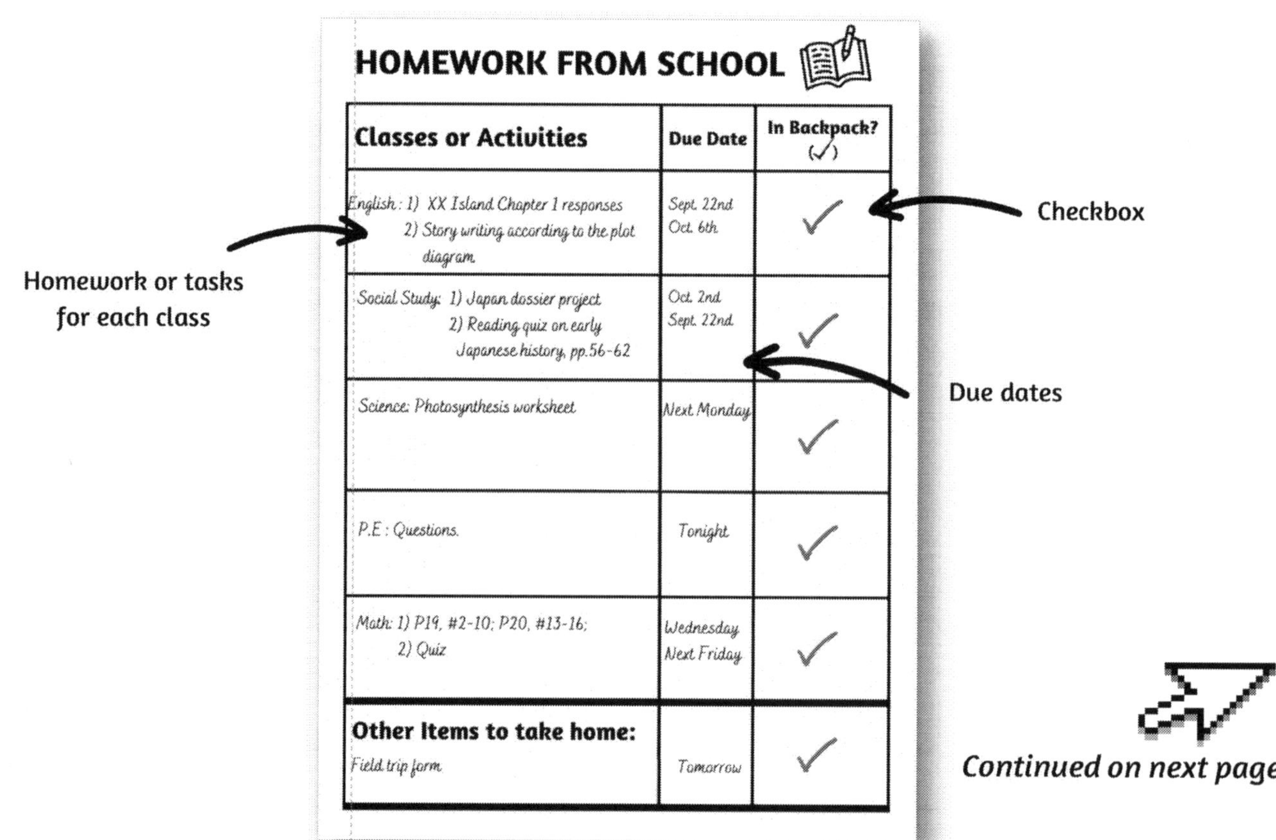

HOMEWORK FROM SCHOOL

Classes or Activities	Due Date	In Backpack? (✓)
English: 1) XX Island Chapter 1 responses 2) Story writing according to the plot diagram	*Sept. 22nd Oct. 6th*	✓
Social Study: 1) Japan dossier project 2) Reading quiz on early Japanese history, pp.56-62	*Oct. 2nd Sept. 22nd*	✓
Science: Photosynthesis worksheet	*Next Monday*	✓
P.E: Questions.	*Tonight*	✓
Math: 1) P19, #2-10; P20, #13-16; 2) Quiz	*Wednesday Next Friday*	✓
Other Items to take home: *Field trip form*	*Tomorrow*	✓

Continued on next page

How to Use This Planner?, Cont.

Step 2- Setting Goals

Find the first Monthly Planner and write down the current month (e.g., September) and its corresponding dates. Follow this process to complete the rest of the months, from October to February. Please see the example below for reference. This planner is designed to cover only six months, making it easily portable and providing ample space to learn new skills. After this initial period, you can switch to the small-sized version to further reinforce the skills learned.

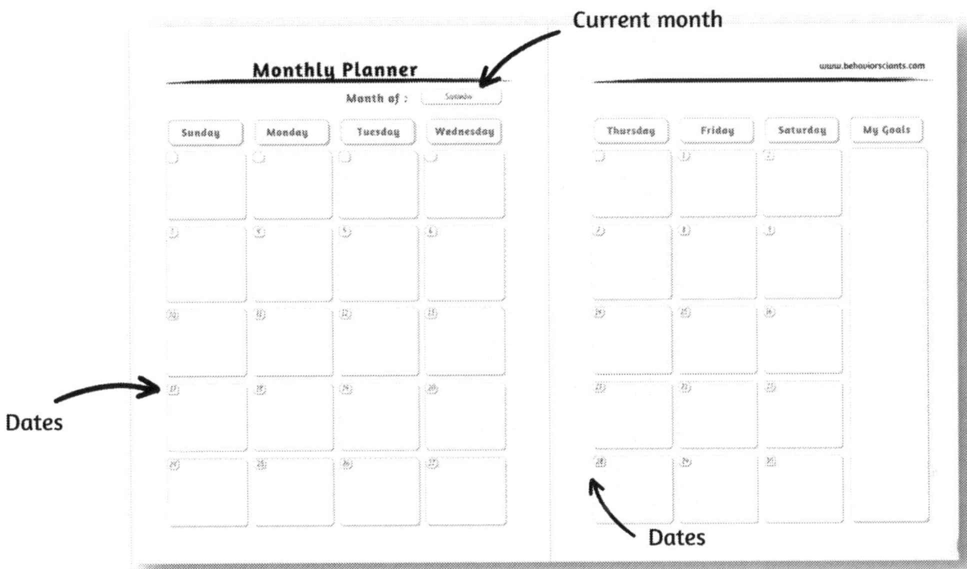

After writing down the months and dates, copy the homework and tasks from the table "HOMEWORK FROM SCHOOL" to the corresponding due dates on the above Monthly Planner(s). Long-term projects may last for more than one week or one month. See the examples below.

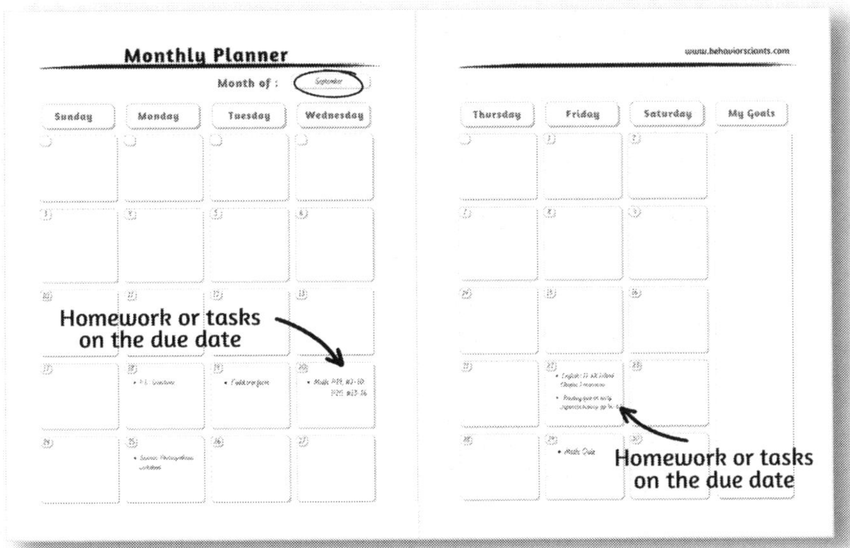

Continued on next page

How to Use This Planner?, Cont.

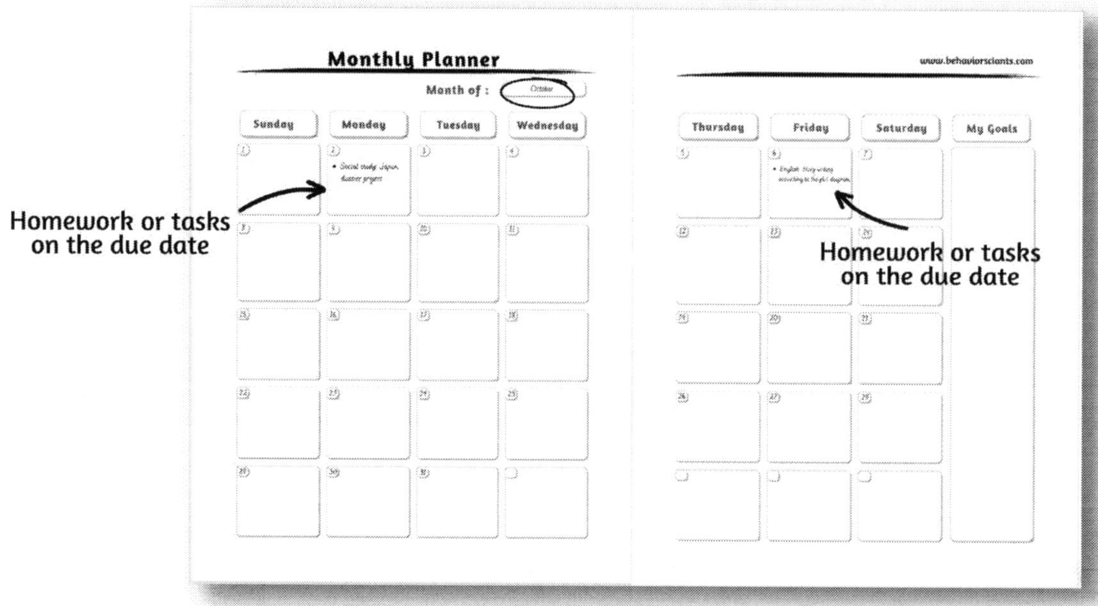

Next, write additional goals to achieve in the corresponding months under the "My Goals" section. See the example below.

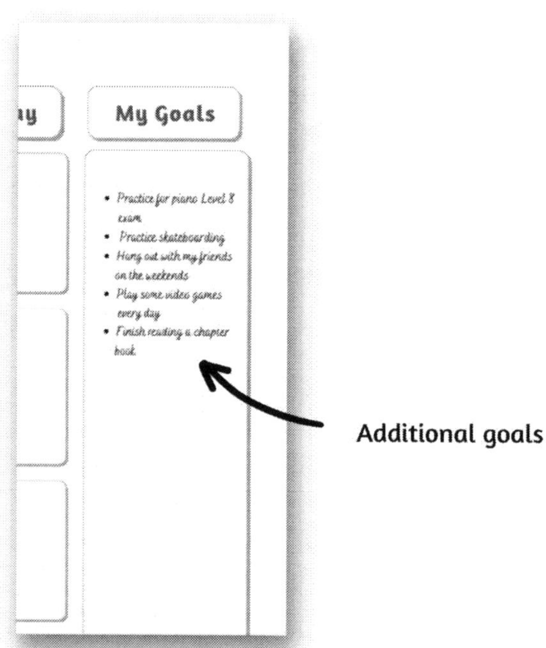

Now, the goals are all set! It's time to move on to the next step!

Continued on next page

How to Use This Planner?, Cont.

Step 3- Planning Backward on the Monthly Planner(s)

For Step 3, start by estimating the time required for each homework or task based on its workload. Then, on the Monthly Planner(s), check the number of days left before the due date. Finally, decide on the days and the amount of time allocated to complete the homework or task each day.

For instance, the math homework is due on September 20th, and it consists of 13 problems (9 problems on p.19 and 4 on p.20). If each problem takes about 15 minutes to solve, you will need approximately 195 minutes (13X15 mins = 195 mins) to complete the entire homework, which is approximately 3.25 hours.

If today is September 18th, you have two days left to work on the math homework before the due date. You can choose to finish it across two days, solving 7 problems on September 18th for about 1.75 hours and the remaining 6 problems on September 19th for about 1.5 hours. Alternatively, you can complete the entire homework in one day, that is, September 18th by solving all 13 problems for 3.25 hours. See the example below.

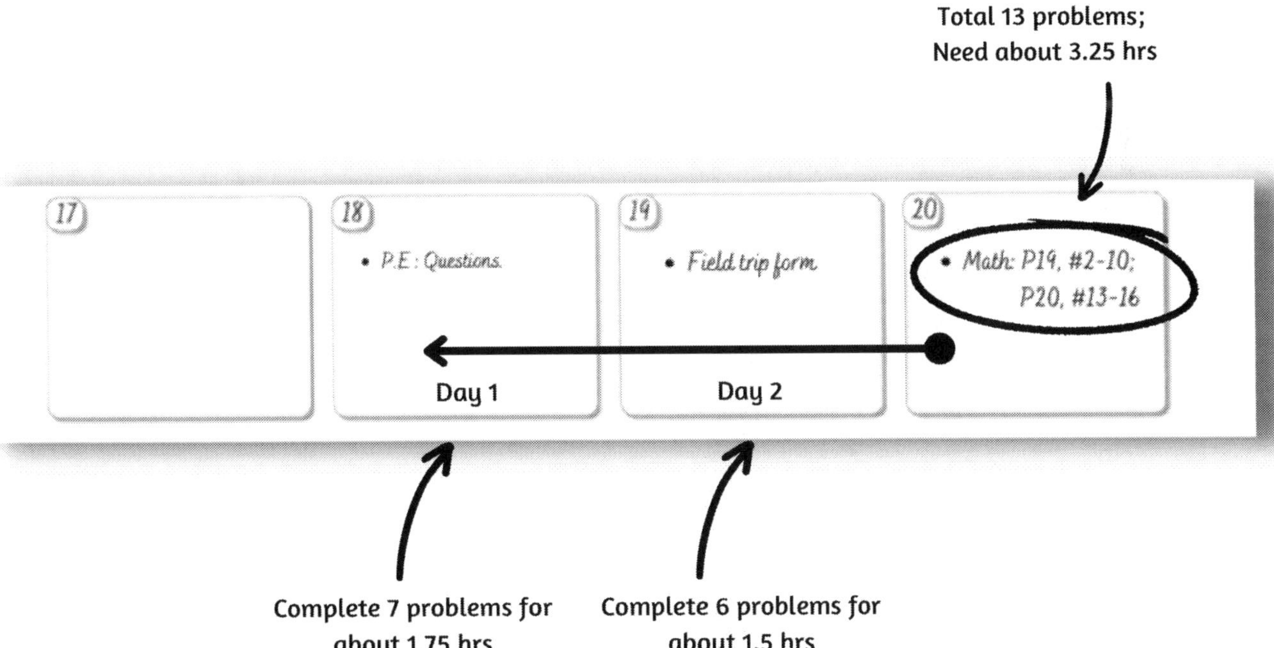

Continued on next page

How to Use This Planner?, Cont.

Step 4- Managing Time

Time management refers to the process of organizing and planning how to divide your time among different activities. Once you have planned your activities on the Monthly Planner(s), transfer the homework, tasks, and other activities of individual dates from the Monthly Planners to the corresponding Daily Planners under the "THINGS TO WORK ON TODAY" section. To get a better understanding, take a look at the example of September 18th provided below.

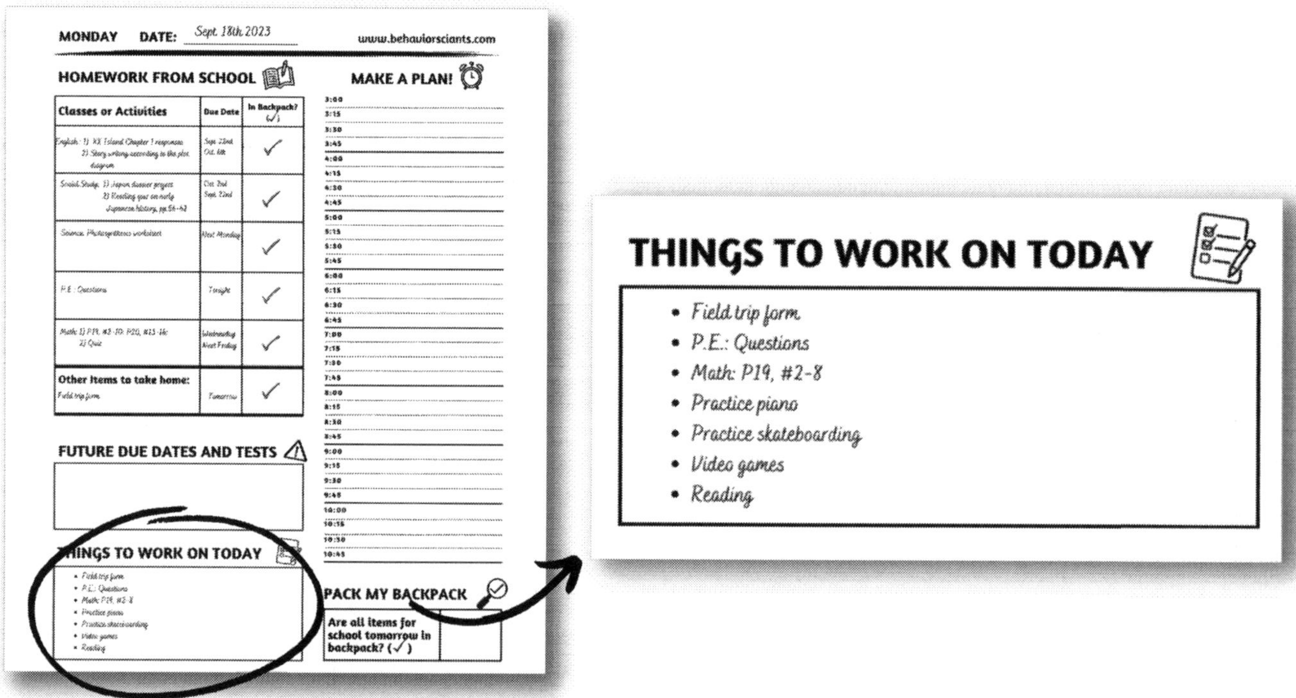

Next, estimate and write down the time needed to complete the homework or tasks, as well as the time you would like to spend on other activities. Refer to the example below for guidance.

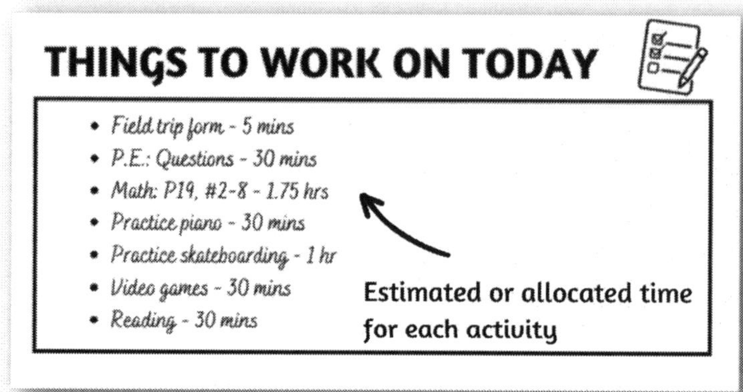

Continued on next page

How to Use This Planner?, Cont.

Step 5- Making a Schedule

Then, it's time to make a schedule based on the items listed in the "THINGS TO WORK ON TODAY" section and their estimated or allocated time. To do this, use the "MAKE A PLAN!" section on the Daily Planner. An example is provided below for reference.

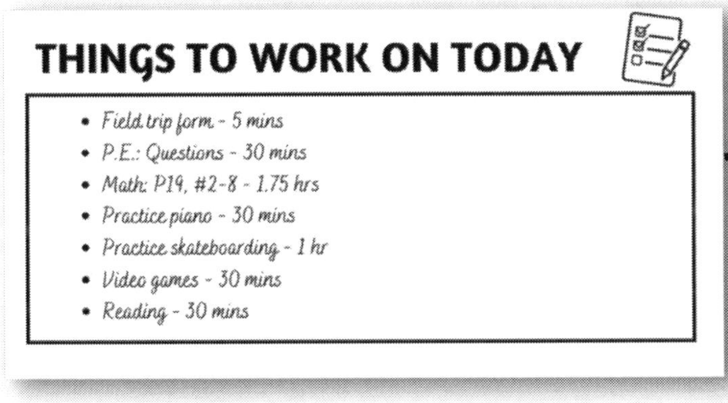

THINGS TO WORK ON TODAY

- *Field trip form - 5 mins*
- *P.E.: Questions - 30 mins*
- *Math: P19, #2-8 - 1.75 hrs*
- *Practice piano - 30 mins*
- *Practice skateboarding - 1 hr*
- *Video games - 30 mins*
- *Reading - 30 mins*

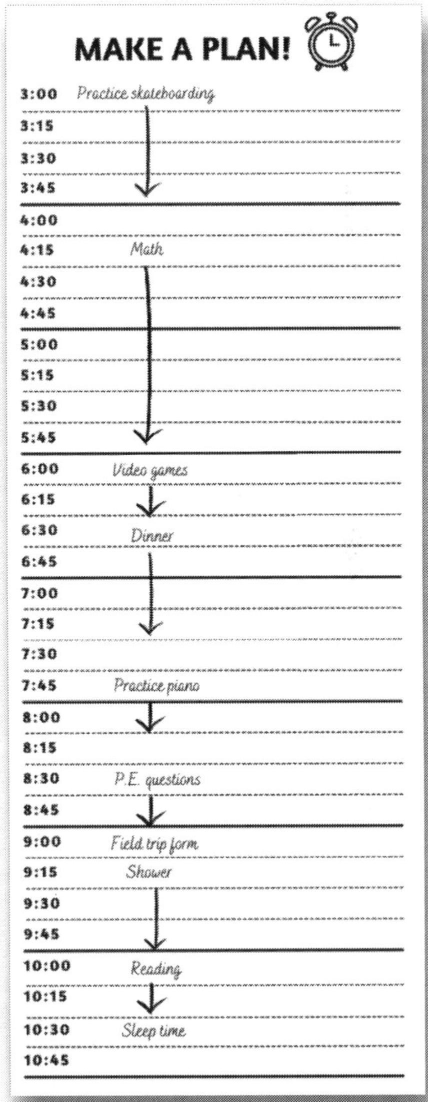

MAKE A PLAN!

3:00	*Practice skateboarding*
3:15	↓
3:30	
3:45	
4:00	
4:15	*Math*
4:30	↓
4:45	
5:00	
5:15	
5:30	
5:45	
6:00	*Video games*
6:15	↓
6:30	*Dinner*
6:45	↓
7:00	
7:15	
7:30	
7:45	*Practice piano*
8:00	↓
8:15	
8:30	*P.E. questions*
8:45	↓
9:00	*Field trip form*
9:15	*Shower*
9:30	↓
9:45	
10:00	*Reading*
10:15	↓
10:30	*Sleep time*
10:45	

Continued on next page

How to Use This Planner?, Cont.

Step 6 - Using Self-Management Strategies to Stay Focused

When following the schedule, you may become distracted. It's important to use self-management strategies to help yourself stay focused. You will need a timer and a token board. Please refer to the section titled "Strategies for Staying Focused" for a detailed procedure.

Step 7 - Solving the problems!

When following the schedule, you may encounter various problems that can distract you from staying on track and prevent you from completing your homework on time. Therefore, it's crucial to have some problem-solving skills. Please refer to the section titled "Situations for Problem-Solving" to learn about common problems you may face and how to solve them in a COOL way.

Step 8 - Packing Your Backpack!

Finally, you have completed all the activities on your schedule! It's time to pack your backpack. Be sure to review the items due the following day on both your Monthly and Daily Planners, and place them in your backpack. Once you've packed everything, tick the box in the lower right corner, as indicated below. You are all set!

Continued on next page

How to Use This Planner?, Cont.

Here is how a completed Daily Planner looks!

MONDAY **DATE:** Sept. 18th 2023 www.behaviorsciants.com

HOMEWORK FROM SCHOOL

Classes or Activities	Due Date	In Backpack? (✓)
English: 1) XX Island Chapter 1 responses 2) Story writing according to the plot diagram	Sept. 22nd Oct. 6th	✓
Social Study: 1) Japan dossier project 2) Reading quiz on early Japanese history, pp.56-62	Oct. 2nd Sept. 22nd	✓
Science: Photosynthesis worksheet	Next Monday	✓
P.E.: Questions	Tonight	✓
Math: 1) P19, #2-10; P20, #13-16; 2) Quiz	Wednesday Next Friday	✓
Other Items to take home: Field trip form	Tomorrow	✓

FUTURE DUE DATES AND TESTS

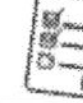

THINGS TO WORK ON TODAY

- Field trip form - 5 mins
- P.E.: Questions - 30 mins
- Math: P19, #2-8 - 1.75 hrs
- Practice piano - 30 mins
- Practice skateboarding - 1 hr
- Video games - 30 mins
- Reading - 30 mins

MAKE A PLAN!

3:00	Practice skateboarding
3:15	↓
3:30	
3:45	
4:00	
4:15	Math
4:30	↓
4:45	
5:00	
5:15	
5:30	
5:45	
6:00	Video games
6:15	↓
6:30	Dinner
6:45	↓
7:00	
7:15	
7:30	
7:45	Practice piano
8:00	↓
8:15	
8:30	P.E. questions
8:45	↓
9:00	Field trip form
9:15	Shower
9:30	↓
9:45	
10:00	Reading
10:15	↓
10:30	Sleep time
10:45	

PACK MY BACKPACK

Are all items for school tomorrow in backpack? (✓)	✓

Strategies for Staying Focused

The diagram below provides strategies for before homework time (antecedent), during homework time (behavior), and as consequences (consequence) to help you identify distractors, arrange the environment to reduce distractors, self-evaluate, self-regulate, and self-reinforce the on-task behavior.

Before doing homework...

- Identify and remove possible distractors, e.g., cell phones, computers, video games, toys, etc.
- Arrange a natural reward right after homework time on the schedule, e.g., 30 minutes of video games after math.
- Set a clear goal for the homework, e.g., complete ____ (number) questions in _____ (time), read ___(number) pages in ___ (time), etc.
- Prepare a timer and token board beside you (See a token board on the next page).

When doing homework...

- Set a timer for 5 minutes or another interval based on how often you get distracted. Evaluate your focus during these intervals throughout your homework time.
- Take a break if needed.
- At the mid-point, check if you have finished half of the work. If yes, you are on the right track! If not, try to speed up!

As consequences ...

- When the timer beeps, if you stayed focused during the interval, draw a ✓ on the token board; if not, draw a X, restart the timer, and try again - stay focused!
- At the end of the designated homework time, if you've finished the work, reward yourself!
- If you haven't finished the work, adjust your plan. You can either (a) work longer, stay more focused, and play less today or (b) work longer and stay more focused the next day.
- If you have more X's than before, reflect on the reasons and make improvements for the next day.

Continued on next page

Strategies for Staying Focused, Cont.

I Can Stay Focused!

My potential distractors:

My goal:

How well can I stay focused?

Interval: ☐ **minutes**

START

FINISH

Total number of ✓ ☐

Total number of X ☐

My reward:

Situations for Problem-Solving

Here are some common situations that involve your problem-solving skills. Please read each situation and use the Problem-Solving Map on the next page to practice solving the problems in a cool way! For a more systematic approach to targeting these skills, please check out the *Learning Problem Solving with Friends* curricula.

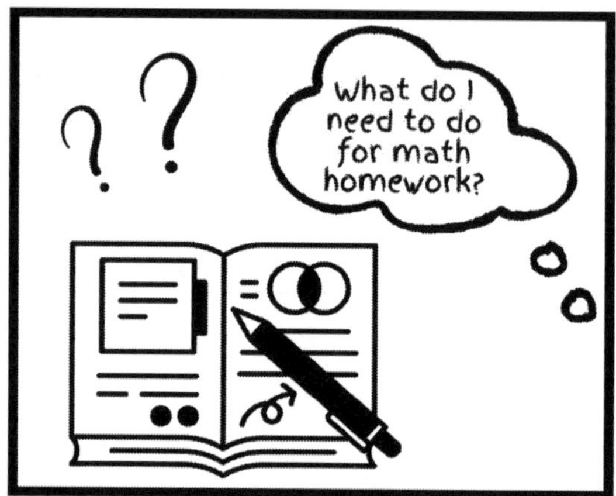

When you try to work on your math homework, you suddenly realize that you forgot to jot down the assignment in your planner. Unfortunately, the due date is tomorrow.

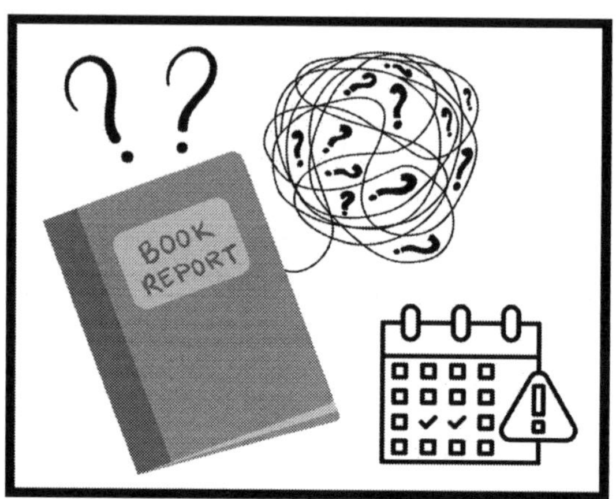

You are working on an English project, but you are stuck. Despite reading through the text and notes, you still can't figure out how to proceed. Unfortunately, you've already spent more time than you planned on this project, and the due date is quickly approaching!

You had planned to spend a lot of time preparing for your Social Studies presentation tomorrow. However, you just got a new game console and really want to try it out today.

You had planned to spend two hours reviewing Chapter 2 for the science quiz tomorrow. However, you got distracted and were not able to finish it within the allotted time. It is currently 9pm and you still have about one-third left to review.

Situations for Problem-Solving, Cont.

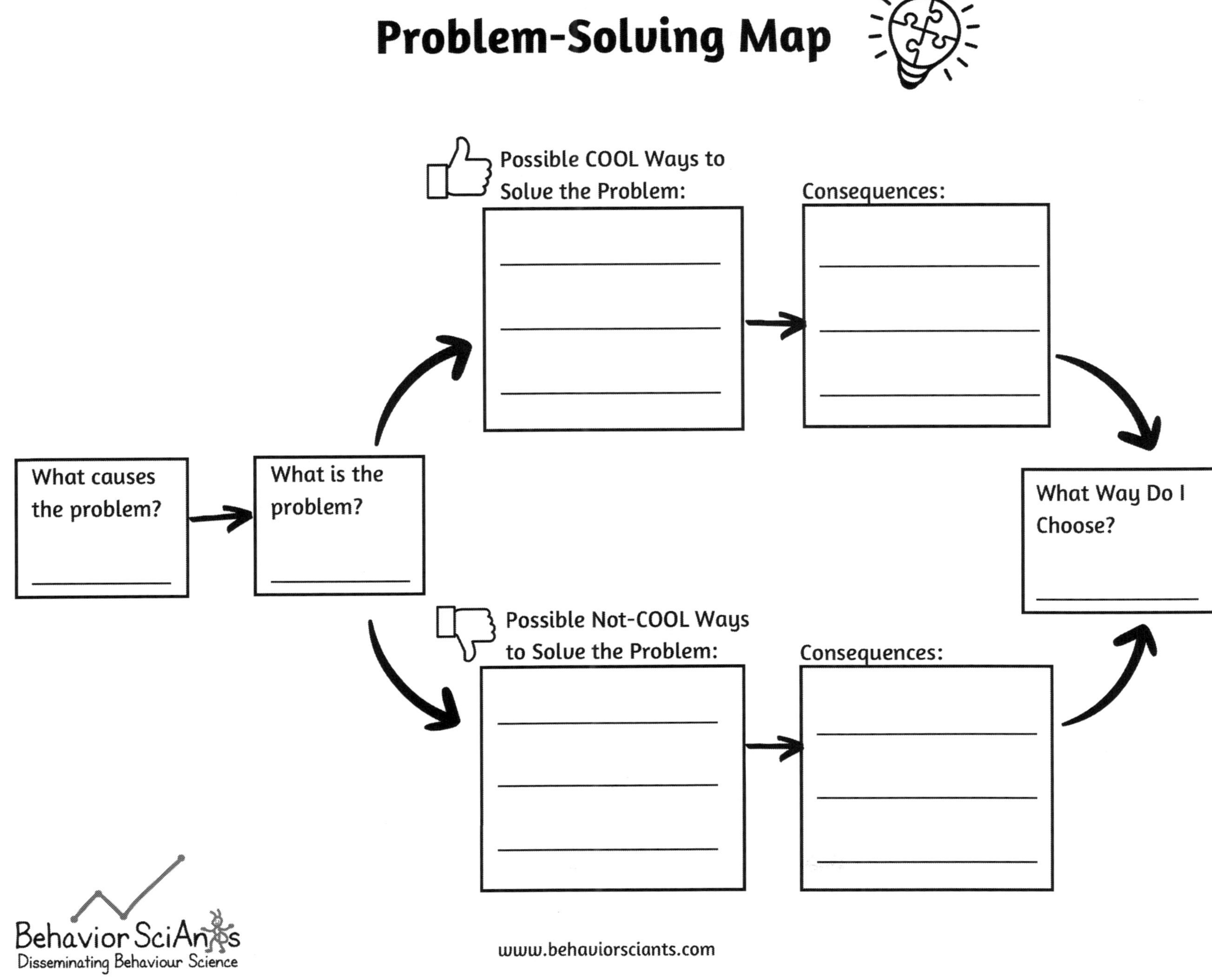

Target List

Targets	Initiation Date	Mastered Date
Taking Notes		
Setting Goals		
Planning backwards on the Monthly Planners		
Managing Time		
Making a Schedule		
Using Self-Management Strategies to Stay Focused		
Solving the Problems		
Packing Backpack		

Monthly Planner

Monthly Planner

Month of :

Sunday	Monday	Tuesday	Wednesday

Thursday	Friday	Saturday	My Goals

Monthly Planner

Month of :

Sunday	Monday	Tuesday	Wednesday

Thursday	Friday	Saturday	My Goals

Monthly Planner

Month of :

Sunday	Monday	Tuesday	Wednesday

Thursday	Friday	Saturday	My Goals

Monthly Planner

Month of :

Sunday	Monday	Tuesday	Wednesday

Thursday	Friday	Saturday	My Goals

Monthly Planner

Month of :

Sunday	Monday	Tuesday	Wednesday

Thursday	Friday	Saturday	My Goals

Monthly Planner

Month of :

Sunday	Monday	Tuesday	Wednesday

Thursday	Friday	Saturday	My Goals

Daily Planner

MONDAY **DATE:** ______________ www.behaviorsciants.com

HOMEWORK FROM SCHOOL 

Classes or Activities	Due Date	In Backpack? (✓)
Other Items to take home:		

FUTURE DUE DATES AND TESTS 

THINGS TO WORK ON TODAY 

MAKE A PLAN! 

3:00
3:15
3:30
3:45
4:00
4:15
4:30
4:45
5:00
5:15
5:30
5:45
6:00
6:15
6:30
6:45
7:00
7:15
7:30
7:45
8:00
8:15
8:30
8:45
9:00
9:15
9:30
9:45
10:00
10:15
10:30
10:45

PACK MY BACKPACK 

Are all items for school tomorrow in backpack? (✓)	

TUESDAY **DATE:** ____________

HOMEWORK FROM SCHOOL

Classes or Activities	Due Date	In Backpack? (✓)
Other Items to take home:		

FUTURE DUE DATES AND TESTS

THINGS TO WORK ON TODAY

MAKE A PLAN!

3:00
3:15
3:30
3:45
4:00
4:15
4:30
4:45
5:00
5:15
5:30
5:45
6:00
6:15
6:30
6:45
7:00
7:15
7:30
7:45
8:00
8:15
8:30
8:45
9:00
9:15
9:30
9:45
10:00
10:15
10:30
10:45

PACK MY BACKPACK

Are all items for school tomorrow in backpack? (✓)	

WEDNESDAY **DATE:** ____________________ www.behaviorsciants.com

HOMEWORK FROM SCHOOL

Classes or Activities	Due Date	In Backpack? (✓)
Other Items to take home:		

FUTURE DUE DATES AND TESTS

THINGS TO WORK ON TODAY

MAKE A PLAN!

3:00
3:15
3:30
3:45
4:00
4:15
4:30
4:45
5:00
5:15
5:30
5:45
6:00
6:15
6:30
6:45
7:00
7:15
7:30
7:45
8:00
8:15
8:30
8:45
9:00
9:15
9:30
9:45
10:00
10:15
10:30
10:45

PACK MY BACKPACK

Are all items for school tomorrow in backpack? (✓)	

THURSDAY DATE: ____________ www.behaviorsciants.com

HOMEWORK FROM SCHOOL

Classes or Activities	Due Date	In Backpack? (✓)
Other Items to take home:		

FUTURE DUE DATES AND TESTS

THINGS TO WORK ON TODAY

MAKE A PLAN!

3:00
3:15
3:30
3:45
4:00
4:15
4:30
4:45
5:00
5:15
5:30
5:45
6:00
6:15
6:30
6:45
7:00
7:15
7:30
7:45
8:00
8:15
8:30
8:45
9:00
9:15
9:30
9:45
10:00
10:15
10:30
10:45

PACK MY BACKPACK

Are all items for school tomorrow in backpack? (✓)	

FRIDAY **DATE:** ____________________ www.behaviorsciants.com

HOMEWORK FROM SCHOOL

Classes or Activities	Due Date	In Backpack? (✓)
Other Items to take home:		

FUTURE DUE DATES AND TESTS

THINGS TO WORK ON TODAY

MAKE A PLAN!

3:00
3:15
3:30
3:45
4:00
4:15
4:30
4:45
5:00
5:15
5:30
5:45
6:00
6:15
6:30
6:45
7:00
7:15
7:30
7:45
8:00
8:15
8:30
8:45
9:00
9:15
9:30
9:45
10:00
10:15
10:30
10:45

PACK MY BACKPACK

Are all items for school tomorrow in backpack? (✓)	

SATURDAY DATE: ____________

MAKE A PLAN! 

9:00
9:30
10:00
10:30
11:00
11:30
12:00
12:30
1:00
1:30
2:00
2:30
3:00
3:30
4:00
4:30
5:00
5:30
6:00
6:30
7:00
7:30
8:00
8:30
9:00
9:30
10:00
10:30
11:00
11:30

THINGS TO WORK ON DURING THE WEEKEND 

SUNDAY DATE: ____________

MAKE A PLAN! 

9:00
9:30
10:00
10:30
11:00
11:30
12:00
12:30
1:00
1:30
2:00
2:30
3:00
3:30
4:00
4:30
5:00
5:30
6:00
6:30
7:00
7:30
8:00
8:30
9:00
9:30
10:00
10:30
11:00
11:30

PACK MY BACKPACK 

Are all items for school tomorrow in backpack? (✓)	

MONDAY DATE: ______________ www.behaviorsciants.com

HOMEWORK FROM SCHOOL

Classes or Activities	Due Date	In Backpack? (✓)
Other Items to take home:		

FUTURE DUE DATES AND TESTS

THINGS TO WORK ON TODAY

MAKE A PLAN!

3:00
3:15
3:30
3:45
4:00
4:15
4:30
4:45
5:00
5:15
5:30
5:45
6:00
6:15
6:30
6:45
7:00
7:15
7:30
7:45
8:00
8:15
8:30
8:45
9:00
9:15
9:30
9:45
10:00
10:15
10:30
10:45

PACK MY BACKPACK

Are all items for school tomorrow in backpack? (✓)	

TUESDAY **DATE:** ____________ www.behaviorsciants.com

HOMEWORK FROM SCHOOL 

Classes or Activities	Due Date	In Backpack? (✓)
Other Items to take home:		

FUTURE DUE DATES AND TESTS

THINGS TO WORK ON TODAY 

MAKE A PLAN! 

3:00
3:15
3:30
3:45
4:00
4:15
4:30
4:45
5:00
5:15
5:30
5:45
6:00
6:15
6:30
6:45
7:00
7:15
7:30
7:45
8:00
8:15
8:30
8:45
9:00
9:15
9:30
9:45
10:00
10:15
10:30
10:45

PACK MY BACKPACK 

Are all items for school tomorrow in backpack? (✓)	

WEDNESDAY **DATE:** ____________________ www.behaviorsciants.com

HOMEWORK FROM SCHOOL

Classes or Activities	Due Date	In Backpack? (✓)
Other Items to take home:		

FUTURE DUE DATES AND TESTS

THINGS TO WORK ON TODAY

MAKE A PLAN!

3:00
3:15
3:30
3:45
4:00
4:15
4:30
4:45
5:00
5:15
5:30
5:45
6:00
6:15
6:30
6:45
7:00
7:15
7:30
7:45
8:00
8:15
8:30
8:45
9:00
9:15
9:30
9:45
10:00
10:15
10:30
10:45

PACK MY BACKPACK

Are all items for school tomorrow in backpack? (✓)	

THURSDAY **DATE:** ______________________ www.behaviorsciants.com

HOMEWORK FROM SCHOOL 

Classes or Activities	Due Date	In Backpack? (✓)
Other Items to take home:		

FUTURE DUE DATES AND TESTS

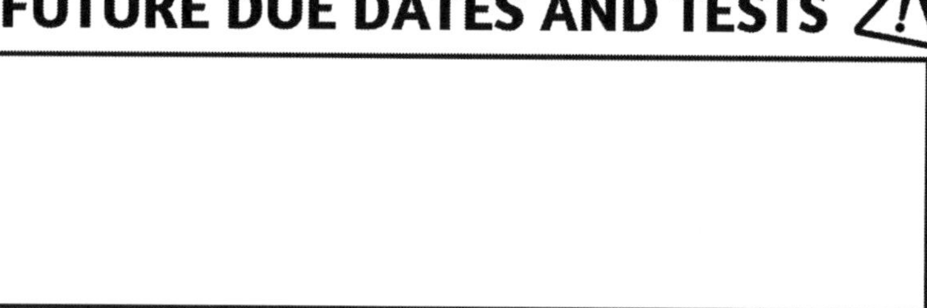

THINGS TO WORK ON TODAY  

MAKE A PLAN! 

3:00
3:15
3:30
3:45
4:00
4:15
4:30
4:45
5:00
5:15
5:30
5:45
6:00
6:15
6:30
6:45
7:00
7:15
7:30
7:45
8:00
8:15
8:30
8:45
9:00
9:15
9:30
9:45
10:00
10:15
10:30
10:45

PACK MY BACKPACK 

Are all items for school tomorrow in backpack? (✓)	

FRIDAY **DATE:** ____________________

HOMEWORK FROM SCHOOL

Classes or Activities	Due Date	In Backpack? (✓)
Other Items to take home:		

FUTURE DUE DATES AND TESTS

THINGS TO WORK ON TODAY

MAKE A PLAN!

3:00
3:15
3:30
3:45
4:00
4:15
4:30
4:45
5:00
5:15
5:30
5:45
6:00
6:15
6:30
6:45
7:00
7:15
7:30
7:45
8:00
8:15
8:30
8:45
9:00
9:15
9:30
9:45
10:00
10:15
10:30
10:45

PACK MY BACKPACK

Are all items for school tomorrow in backpack? (✓)	

SATURDAY DATE: ____________

MAKE A PLAN!

9:00
9:30
10:00
10:30
11:00
11:30
12:00
12:30
1:00
1:30
2:00
2:30
3:00
3:30
4:00
4:30
5:00
5:30
6:00
6:30
7:00
7:30
8:00
8:30
9:00
9:30
10:00
10:30
11:00
11:30

THINGS TO WORK ON DURING THE WEEKEND

SUNDAY DATE: ____________

MAKE A PLAN!

9:00
9:30
10:00
10:30
11:00
11:30
12:00
12:30
1:00
1:30
2:00
2:30
3:00
3:30
4:00
4:30
5:00
5:30
6:00
6:30
7:00
7:30
8:00
8:30
9:00
9:30
10:00
10:30
11:00
11:30

PACK MY BACKPACK

Are all items for school tomorrow in backpack? (✓)	

MONDAY DATE: ________________ www.behaviorsciants.com

HOMEWORK FROM SCHOOL

Classes or Activities	Due Date	In Backpack? (✓)
Other Items to take home:		

FUTURE DUE DATES AND TESTS

THINGS TO WORK ON TODAY

MAKE A PLAN!

3:00
3:15
3:30
3:45
4:00
4:15
4:30
4:45
5:00
5:15
5:30
5:45
6:00
6:15
6:30
6:45
7:00
7:15
7:30
7:45
8:00
8:15
8:30
8:45
9:00
9:15
9:30
9:45
10:00
10:15
10:30
10:45

PACK MY BACKPACK

Are all items for school tomorrow in backpack? (✓)	

TUESDAY **DATE:** ____________________ www.behaviorsciants.com

HOMEWORK FROM SCHOOL 

Classes or Activities	Due Date	In Backpack? (✓)
Other Items to take home:		

MAKE A PLAN! 

3:00
3:15
3:30
3:45
4:00
4:15
4:30
4:45
5:00
5:15
5:30
5:45
6:00
6:15
6:30
6:45
7:00
7:15
7:30
7:45
8:00
8:15
8:30
8:45
9:00
9:15
9:30
9:45
10:00
10:15
10:30
10:45

FUTURE DUE DATES AND TESTS

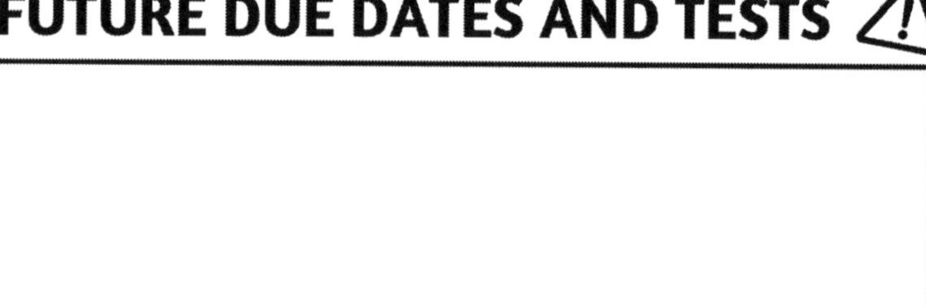

THINGS TO WORK ON TODAY 

PACK MY BACKPACK 

Are all items for school tomorrow in backpack? (✓)	

WEDNESDAY **DATE:** ____________ www.behaviorsciants.com

HOMEWORK FROM SCHOOL

Classes or Activities	Due Date	In Backpack? (✓)
Other Items to take home:		

FUTURE DUE DATES AND TESTS

THINGS TO WORK ON TODAY

MAKE A PLAN!

3:00	
3:15	
3:30	
3:45	
4:00	
4:15	
4:30	
4:45	
5:00	
5:15	
5:30	
5:45	
6:00	
6:15	
6:30	
6:45	
7:00	
7:15	
7:30	
7:45	
8:00	
8:15	
8:30	
8:45	
9:00	
9:15	
9:30	
9:45	
10:00	
10:15	
10:30	
10:45	

PACK MY BACKPACK

Are all items for school tomorrow in backpack? (✓)	

THURSDAY **DATE:** ______________ www.behaviorsciants.com

HOMEWORK FROM SCHOOL

Classes or Activities	Due Date	In Backpack? (✓)
Other Items to take home:		

FUTURE DUE DATES AND TESTS

THINGS TO WORK ON TODAY

MAKE A PLAN!

3:00
3:15
3:30
3:45
4:00
4:15
4:30
4:45
5:00
5:15
5:30
5:45
6:00
6:15
6:30
6:45
7:00
7:15
7:30
7:45
8:00
8:15
8:30
8:45
9:00
9:15
9:30
9:45
10:00
10:15
10:30
10:45

PACK MY BACKPACK

Are all items for school tomorrow in backpack? (✓)	

FRIDAY **DATE:** ____________

www.behaviorsciants.com

HOMEWORK FROM SCHOOL

Classes or Activities	Due Date	In Backpack? (✓)
Other Items to take home:		

FUTURE DUE DATES AND TESTS

THINGS TO WORK ON TODAY

MAKE A PLAN!

3:00
3:15
3:30
3:45
4:00
4:15
4:30
4:45
5:00
5:15
5:30
5:45
6:00
6:15
6:30
6:45
7:00
7:15
7:30
7:45
8:00
8:15
8:30
8:45
9:00
9:15
9:30
9:45
10:00
10:15
10:30
10:45

PACK MY BACKPACK

Are all items for school tomorrow in backpack? (✓)	

SATURDAY DATE: ____________

MAKE A PLAN! 

9:00
9:30
10:00
10:30
11:00
11:30
12:00
12:30
1:00
1:30
2:00
2:30
3:00
3:30
4:00
4:30
5:00
5:30
6:00
6:30
7:00
7:30
8:00
8:30
9:00
9:30
10:00
10:30
11:00
11:30

THINGS TO WORK ON DURING THE WEEKEND 

SUNDAY DATE: ____________

MAKE A PLAN! 

9:00
9:30
10:00
10:30
11:00
11:30
12:00
12:30
1:00
1:30
2:00
2:30
3:00
3:30
4:00
4:30
5:00
5:30
6:00
6:30
7:00
7:30
8:00
8:30
9:00
9:30
10:00
10:30
11:00
11:30

PACK MY BACKPACK 

Are all items for school tomorrow in backpack? (✓)	

MONDAY **DATE:** ______________ www.behaviorsciants.com

HOMEWORK FROM SCHOOL 

Classes or Activities	Due Date	In Backpack? (✓)
Other Items to take home:		

FUTURE DUE DATES AND TESTS 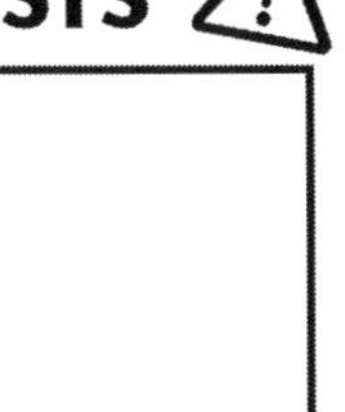

THINGS TO WORK ON TODAY  

MAKE A PLAN! 

3:00
3:15
3:30
3:45
4:00
4:15
4:30
4:45
5:00
5:15
5:30
5:45
6:00
6:15
6:30
6:45
7:00
7:15
7:30
7:45
8:00
8:15
8:30
8:45
9:00
9:15
9:30
9:45
10:00
10:15
10:30
10:45

PACK MY BACKPACK 

Are all items for school tomorrow in backpack? (✓)	

TUESDAY **DATE:** ____________________

HOMEWORK FROM SCHOOL

Classes or Activities	Due Date	In Backpack? (✓)
Other Items to take home:		

FUTURE DUE DATES AND TESTS

THINGS TO WORK ON TODAY

MAKE A PLAN!

3:00

3:15

3:30

3:45

4:00

4:15

4:30

4:45

5:00

5:15

5:30

5:45

6:00

6:15

6:30

6:45

7:00

7:15

7:30

7:45

8:00

8:15

8:30

8:45

9:00

9:15

9:30

9:45

10:00

10:15

10:30

10:45

PACK MY BACKPACK

Are all items for school tomorrow in backpack? (✓)	

WEDNESDAY DATE: ____________ www.behaviorsciants.com

HOMEWORK FROM SCHOOL

Classes or Activities	Due Date	In Backpack? (✓)
Other Items to take home:		

FUTURE DUE DATES AND TESTS

THINGS TO WORK ON TODAY

MAKE A PLAN!

3:00
3:15
3:30
3:45
4:00
4:15
4:30
4:45
5:00
5:15
5:30
5:45
6:00
6:15
6:30
6:45
7:00
7:15
7:30
7:45
8:00
8:15
8:30
8:45
9:00
9:15
9:30
9:45
10:00
10:15
10:30
10:45

PACK MY BACKPACK

Are all items for school tomorrow in backpack? (✓)	

THURSDAY **DATE:** ____________________ www.behaviorsciants.com

HOMEWORK FROM SCHOOL 

Classes or Activities	Due Date	In Backpack? (✓)
Other Items to take home:		

FUTURE DUE DATES AND TESTS

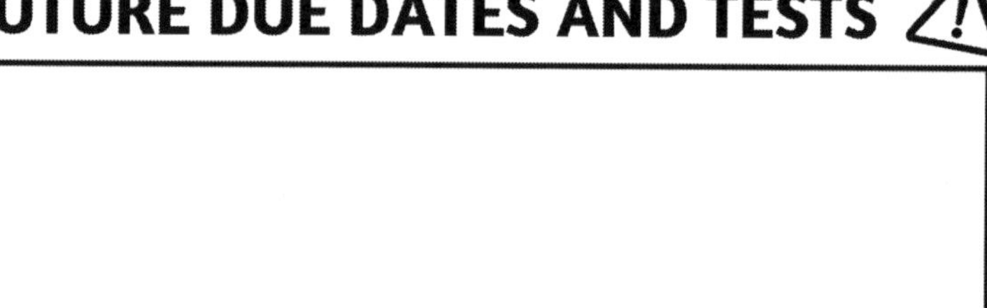

THINGS TO WORK ON TODAY 

MAKE A PLAN! 

3:00
3:15
3:30
3:45
4:00
4:15
4:30
4:45
5:00
5:15
5:30
5:45
6:00
6:15
6:30
6:45
7:00
7:15
7:30
7:45
8:00
8:15
8:30
8:45
9:00
9:15
9:30
9:45
10:00
10:15
10:30
10:45

PACK MY BACKPACK 

Are all items for school tomorrow in backpack? (✓)	

FRIDAY **DATE:** ____________________ www.behaviorsciants.com

HOMEWORK FROM SCHOOL

Classes or Activities	Due Date	In Backpack? (✓)
Other Items to take home:		

FUTURE DUE DATES AND TESTS

THINGS TO WORK ON TODAY

MAKE A PLAN!

3:00
3:15
3:30
3:45
4:00
4:15
4:30
4:45
5:00
5:15
5:30
5:45
6:00
6:15
6:30
6:45
7:00
7:15
7:30
7:45
8:00
8:15
8:30
8:45
9:00
9:15
9:30
9:45
10:00
10:15
10:30
10:45

PACK MY BACKPACK

Are all items for school tomorrow in backpack? (✓)	

SATURDAY DATE: ______

MAKE A PLAN!

9:00
9:30
10:00
10:30
11:00
11:30
12:00
12:30
1:00
1:30
2:00
2:30
3:00
3:30
4:00
4:30
5:00
5:30
6:00
6:30
7:00
7:30
8:00
8:30
9:00
9:30
10:00
10:30
11:00
11:30

THINGS TO WORK ON DURING THE WEEKEND

SUNDAY DATE: ______

MAKE A PLAN!

9:00
9:30
10:00
10:30
11:00
11:30
12:00
12:30
1:00
1:30
2:00
2:30
3:00
3:30
4:00
4:30
5:00
5:30
6:00
6:30
7:00
7:30
8:00
8:30
9:00
9:30
10:00
10:30
11:00
11:30

PACK MY BACKPACK

Are all items for school tomorrow in backpack? (✓)	

MONDAY **DATE:** ____________ www.behaviorsciants.com

HOMEWORK FROM SCHOOL 

Classes or Activities	Due Date	In Backpack? (✓)
Other Items to take home:		

FUTURE DUE DATES AND TESTS

THINGS TO WORK ON TODAY

MAKE A PLAN! 

3:00
3:15
3:30
3:45
4:00
4:15
4:30
4:45
5:00
5:15
5:30
5:45
6:00
6:15
6:30
6:45
7:00
7:15
7:30
7:45
8:00
8:15
8:30
8:45
9:00
9:15
9:30
9:45
10:00
10:15
10:30
10:45

PACK MY BACKPACK 

Are all items for school tomorrow in backpack? (✓)	

TUESDAY **DATE:** ____________

www.behaviorsciants.com

HOMEWORK FROM SCHOOL

Classes or Activities	Due Date	In Backpack? (✓)
Other Items to take home:		

FUTURE DUE DATES AND TESTS

THINGS TO WORK ON TODAY

MAKE A PLAN!

3:00
3:15
3:30
3:45
4:00
4:15
4:30
4:45
5:00
5:15
5:30
5:45
6:00
6:15
6:30
6:45
7:00
7:15
7:30
7:45
8:00
8:15
8:30
8:45
9:00
9:15
9:30
9:45
10:00
10:15
10:30
10:45

PACK MY BACKPACK

Are all items for school tomorrow in backpack? (✓)	

WEDNESDAY **DATE:** ____________________ www.behaviorsciants.com

HOMEWORK FROM SCHOOL

Classes or Activities	Due Date	In Backpack? (✓)
Other Items to take home:		

FUTURE DUE DATES AND TESTS

THINGS TO WORK ON TODAY

MAKE A PLAN!

3:00
3:15
3:30
3:45
4:00
4:15
4:30
4:45
5:00
5:15
5:30
5:45
6:00
6:15
6:30
6:45
7:00
7:15
7:30
7:45
8:00
8:15
8:30
8:45
9:00
9:15
9:30
9:45
10:00
10:15
10:30
10:45

PACK MY BACKPACK

Are all items for school tomorrow in backpack? (✓)	

THURSDAY **DATE:** ____________________

www.behaviorsciants.com

HOMEWORK FROM SCHOOL

Classes or Activities	Due Date	In Backpack? (✓)
Other Items to take home:		

FUTURE DUE DATES AND TESTS

THINGS TO WORK ON TODAY

MAKE A PLAN!

3:00

3:15

3:30

3:45

4:00

4:15

4:30

4:45

5:00

5:15

5:30

5:45

6:00

6:15

6:30

6:45

7:00

7:15

7:30

7:45

8:00

8:15

8:30

8:45

9:00

9:15

9:30

9:45

10:00

10:15

10:30

10:45

PACK MY BACKPACK

Are all items for school tomorrow in backpack? (✓)	

FRIDAY **DATE:** ____________ www.behaviorsciants.com

HOMEWORK FROM SCHOOL

Classes or Activities	Due Date	In Backpack? (✓)
Other Items to take home:		

FUTURE DUE DATES AND TESTS

THINGS TO WORK ON TODAY

MAKE A PLAN!

3:00
3:15
3:30
3:45
4:00
4:15
4:30
4:45
5:00
5:15
5:30
5:45
6:00
6:15
6:30
6:45
7:00
7:15
7:30
7:45
8:00
8:15
8:30
8:45
9:00
9:15
9:30
9:45
10:00
10:15
10:30
10:45

PACK MY BACKPACK

Are all items for school tomorrow in backpack? (✓)	

SATURDAY DATE: ______

MAKE A PLAN!

9:00
9:30
10:00
10:30
11:00
11:30
12:00
12:30
1:00
1:30
2:00
2:30
3:00
3:30
4:00
4:30
5:00
5:30
6:00
6:30
7:00
7:30
8:00
8:30
9:00
9:30
10:00
10:30
11:00
11:30

THINGS TO WORK ON DURING THE WEEKEND

SUNDAY DATE: ______

MAKE A PLAN!

9:00
9:30
10:00
10:30
11:00
11:30
12:00
12:30
1:00
1:30
2:00
2:30
3:00
3:30
4:00
4:30
5:00
5:30
6:00
6:30
7:00
7:30
8:00
8:30
9:00
9:30
10:00
10:30
11:00
11:30

PACK MY BACKPACK

Are all items for school tomorrow in backpack? (✓)	

MONDAY **DATE:** ____________________ www.behaviorsciants.com

HOMEWORK FROM SCHOOL

Classes or Activities	Due Date	In Backpack? (✓)
Other Items to take home:		

FUTURE DUE DATES AND TESTS

THINGS TO WORK ON TODAY

MAKE A PLAN!

3:00
3:15
3:30
3:45
4:00
4:15
4:30
4:45
5:00
5:15
5:30
5:45
6:00
6:15
6:30
6:45
7:00
7:15
7:30
7:45
8:00
8:15
8:30
8:45
9:00
9:15
9:30
9:45
10:00
10:15
10:30
10:45

PACK MY BACKPACK

Are all items for school tomorrow in backpack? (✓)	

TUESDAY **DATE:** ____________________

www.behaviorsciants.com

HOMEWORK FROM SCHOOL

Classes or Activities	Due Date	In Backpack? (✓)
Other Items to take home:		

FUTURE DUE DATES AND TESTS

THINGS TO WORK ON TODAY

MAKE A PLAN!

3:00
3:15
3:30
3:45
4:00
4:15
4:30
4:45
5:00
5:15
5:30
5:45
6:00
6:15
6:30
6:45
7:00
7:15
7:30
7:45
8:00
8:15
8:30
8:45
9:00
9:15
9:30
9:45
10:00
10:15
10:30
10:45

PACK MY BACKPACK

Are all items for school tomorrow in backpack? (✓)	

WEDNESDAY **DATE:** ______________ www.behaviorsciants.com

HOMEWORK FROM SCHOOL

Classes or Activities	Due Date	In Backpack? (✓)
Other Items to take home:		

FUTURE DUE DATES AND TESTS

THINGS TO WORK ON TODAY

MAKE A PLAN!

3:00
3:15
3:30
3:45
4:00
4:15
4:30
4:45
5:00
5:15
5:30
5:45
6:00
6:15
6:30
6:45
7:00
7:15
7:30
7:45
8:00
8:15
8:30
8:45
9:00
9:15
9:30
9:45
10:00
10:15
10:30
10:45

PACK MY BACKPACK

Are all items for school tomorrow in backpack? (✓)	

THURSDAY **DATE:** ____________________ www.behaviorsciants.com

HOMEWORK FROM SCHOOL

Classes or Activities	Due Date	In Backpack? (✓)
Other Items to take home:		

FUTURE DUE DATES AND TESTS

THINGS TO WORK ON TODAY

MAKE A PLAN!

3:00
3:15
3:30
3:45
4:00
4:15
4:30
4:45
5:00
5:15
5:30
5:45
6:00
6:15
6:30
6:45
7:00
7:15
7:30
7:45
8:00
8:15
8:30
8:45
9:00
9:15
9:30
9:45
10:00
10:15
10:30
10:45

PACK MY BACKPACK

Are all items for school tomorrow in backpack? (✓)	

FRIDAY **DATE:** ____________

www.behaviorsciants.com

HOMEWORK FROM SCHOOL

Classes or Activities	Due Date	In Backpack? (✓)
Other Items to take home:		

FUTURE DUE DATES AND TESTS

THINGS TO WORK ON TODAY

MAKE A PLAN!

3:00	
3:15	
3:30	
3:45	
4:00	
4:15	
4:30	
4:45	
5:00	
5:15	
5:30	
5:45	
6:00	
6:15	
6:30	
6:45	
7:00	
7:15	
7:30	
7:45	
8:00	
8:15	
8:30	
8:45	
9:00	
9:15	
9:30	
9:45	
10:00	
10:15	
10:30	
10:45	

PACK MY BACKPACK

Are all items for school tomorrow in backpack? (✓)	

SATURDAY DATE: ____________

MAKE A PLAN! 

9:00
9:30
10:00
10:30
11:00
11:30
12:00
12:30
1:00
1:30
2:00
2:30
3:00
3:30
4:00
4:30
5:00
5:30
6:00
6:30
7:00
7:30
8:00
8:30
9:00
9:30
10:00
10:30
11:00
11:30

THINGS TO WORK ON DURING THE WEEKEND 

SUNDAY DATE: ____________

MAKE A PLAN! 

9:00
9:30
10:00
10:30
11:00
11:30
12:00
12:30
1:00
1:30
2:00
2:30
3:00
3:30
4:00
4:30
5:00
5:30
6:00
6:30
7:00
7:30
8:00
8:30
9:00
9:30
10:00
10:30
11:00
11:30

PACK MY BACKPACK 

Are all items for school tomorrow in backpack? (✓)	

MONDAY DATE: ____________ www.behaviorsciants.com

HOMEWORK FROM SCHOOL 

Classes or Activities	Due Date	In Backpack? (✓)
Other Items to take home:		

FUTURE DUE DATES AND TESTS

THINGS TO WORK ON TODAY

MAKE A PLAN! 

3:00
3:15
3:30
3:45
4:00
4:15
4:30
4:45
5:00
5:15
5:30
5:45
6:00
6:15
6:30
6:45
7:00
7:15
7:30
7:45
8:00
8:15
8:30
8:45
9:00
9:15
9:30
9:45
10:00
10:15
10:30
10:45

PACK MY BACKPACK

Are all items for school tomorrow in backpack? (✓)	

TUESDAY **DATE:** ____________________ www.behaviorsciants.com

HOMEWORK FROM SCHOOL 

Classes or Activities	Due Date	In Backpack? (✓)
Other Items to take home:		

FUTURE DUE DATES AND TESTS

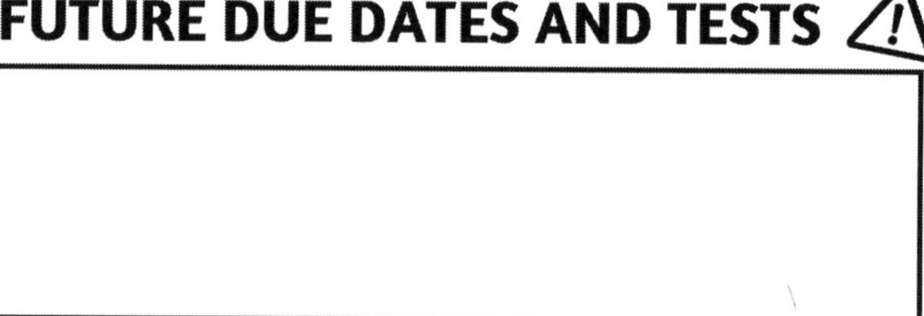

THINGS TO WORK ON TODAY 

MAKE A PLAN! 

3:00
3:15
3:30
3:45
4:00
4:15
4:30
4:45
5:00
5:15
5:30
5:45
6:00
6:15
6:30
6:45
7:00
7:15
7:30
7:45
8:00
8:15
8:30
8:45
9:00
9:15
9:30
9:45
10:00
10:15
10:30
10:45

PACK MY BACKPACK 

Are all items for school tomorrow in backpack? (✓)	

WEDNESDAY **DATE:** ____________________ www.behaviorsciants.com

HOMEWORK FROM SCHOOL 

Classes or Activities	Due Date	In Backpack? (✓)
Other Items to take home:		

FUTURE DUE DATES AND TESTS

THINGS TO WORK ON TODAY 

MAKE A PLAN! 

3:00
3:15
3:30
3:45
4:00
4:15
4:30
4:45
5:00
5:15
5:30
5:45
6:00
6:15
6:30
6:45
7:00
7:15
7:30
7:45
8:00
8:15
8:30
8:45
9:00
9:15
9:30
9:45
10:00
10:15
10:30
10:45

PACK MY BACKPACK 

Are all items for school tomorrow in backpack? (✓)	

THURSDAY **DATE:** ____________________

www.behaviorsciants.com

HOMEWORK FROM SCHOOL

Classes or Activities	Due Date	In Backpack? (✓)
Other Items to take home:		

FUTURE DUE DATES AND TESTS

THINGS TO WORK ON TODAY

MAKE A PLAN!

3:00
3:15
3:30
3:45
4:00
4:15
4:30
4:45
5:00
5:15
5:30
5:45
6:00
6:15
6:30
6:45
7:00
7:15
7:30
7:45
8:00
8:15
8:30
8:45
9:00
9:15
9:30
9:45
10:00
10:15
10:30
10:45

PACK MY BACKPACK

Are all items for school tomorrow in backpack? (✓)	

FRIDAY **DATE:** ____________________ www.behaviorsciants.com

HOMEWORK FROM SCHOOL

Classes or Activities	Due Date	In Backpack? (✓)
Other Items to take home:		

FUTURE DUE DATES AND TESTS

THINGS TO WORK ON TODAY

MAKE A PLAN!

3:00
3:15
3:30
3:45
4:00
4:15
4:30
4:45
5:00
5:15
5:30
5:45
6:00
6:15
6:30
6:45
7:00
7:15
7:30
7:45
8:00
8:15
8:30
8:45
9:00
9:15
9:30
9:45
10:00
10:15
10:30
10:45

PACK MY BACKPACK

Are all items for school tomorrow in backpack? (✓)	

SATURDAY DATE: ____________

MAKE A PLAN!

9:00
9:30
10:00
10:30
11:00
11:30
12:00
12:30
1:00
1:30
2:00
2:30
3:00
3:30
4:00
4:30
5:00
5:30
6:00
6:30
7:00
7:30
8:00
8:30
9:00
9:30
10:00
10:30
11:00
11:30

THINGS TO WORK ON DURING THE WEEKEND

SUNDAY DATE: ____________

MAKE A PLAN!

9:00
9:30
10:00
10:30
11:00
11:30
12:00
12:30
1:00
1:30
2:00
2:30
3:00
3:30
4:00
4:30
5:00
5:30
6:00
6:30
7:00
7:30
8:00
8:30
9:00
9:30
10:00
10:30
11:00
11:30

PACK MY BACKPACK

Are all items for school tomorrow in backpack? (✓)	

MONDAY **DATE:** ____________________ www.behaviorsciants.com

HOMEWORK FROM SCHOOL 

Classes or Activities	Due Date	In Backpack? (✓)
Other Items to take home:		

FUTURE DUE DATES AND TESTS

THINGS TO WORK ON TODAY

MAKE A PLAN! 

3:00
3:15
3:30
3:45
4:00
4:15
4:30
4:45
5:00
5:15
5:30
5:45
6:00
6:15
6:30
6:45
7:00
7:15
7:30
7:45
8:00
8:15
8:30
8:45
9:00
9:15
9:30
9:45
10:00
10:15
10:30
10:45

PACK MY BACKPACK 

Are all items for school tomorrow in backpack? (✓)	

TUESDAY **DATE:** ____________ www.behaviorsciants.com

HOMEWORK FROM SCHOOL

Classes or Activities	Due Date	In Backpack? (✓)
Other Items to take home:		

FUTURE DUE DATES AND TESTS

THINGS TO WORK ON TODAY

MAKE A PLAN!

3:00
3:15
3:30
3:45
4:00
4:15
4:30
4:45
5:00
5:15
5:30
5:45
6:00
6:15
6:30
6:45
7:00
7:15
7:30
7:45
8:00
8:15
8:30
8:45
9:00
9:15
9:30
9:45
10:00
10:15
10:30
10:45

PACK MY BACKPACK

Are all items for school tomorrow in backpack? (✓)	

WEDNESDAY **DATE:** ____________________ www.behaviorsciants.com

HOMEWORK FROM SCHOOL

Classes or Activities	Due Date	In Backpack? (✓)
Other Items to take home:		

FUTURE DUE DATES AND TESTS

THINGS TO WORK ON TODAY

MAKE A PLAN!

3:00
3:15
3:30
3:45
4:00
4:15
4:30
4:45
5:00
5:15
5:30
5:45
6:00
6:15
6:30
6:45
7:00
7:15
7:30
7:45
8:00
8:15
8:30
8:45
9:00
9:15
9:30
9:45
10:00
10:15
10:30
10:45

PACK MY BACKPACK

Are all items for school tomorrow in backpack? (✓)	

THURSDAY **DATE:** ____________

www.behaviorsciants.com

HOMEWORK FROM SCHOOL

Classes or Activities	Due Date	In Backpack? (✓)
Other Items to take home:		

FUTURE DUE DATES AND TESTS

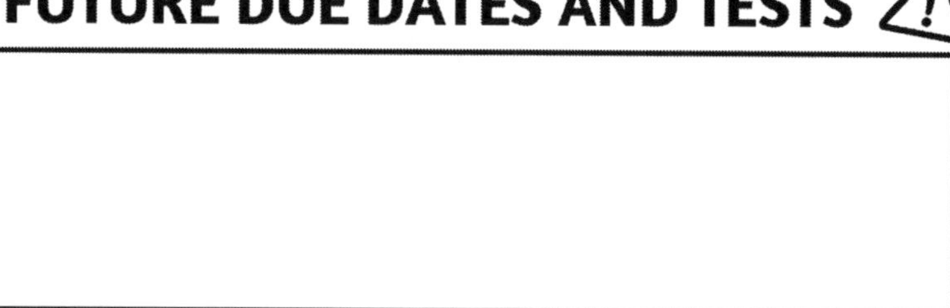

THINGS TO WORK ON TODAY

MAKE A PLAN!

3:00	
3:15	
3:30	
3:45	
4:00	
4:15	
4:30	
4:45	
5:00	
5:15	
5:30	
5:45	
6:00	
6:15	
6:30	
6:45	
7:00	
7:15	
7:30	
7:45	
8:00	
8:15	
8:30	
8:45	
9:00	
9:15	
9:30	
9:45	
10:00	
10:15	
10:30	
10:45	

PACK MY BACKPACK

Are all items for school tomorrow in backpack? (✓)	

FRIDAY **DATE:** ____________ www.behaviorsciants.com

HOMEWORK FROM SCHOOL

Classes or Activities	Due Date	In Backpack? (✓)
Other Items to take home:		

FUTURE DUE DATES AND TESTS

THINGS TO WORK ON TODAY

MAKE A PLAN!

3:00
3:15
3:30
3:45
4:00
4:15
4:30
4:45
5:00
5:15
5:30
5:45
6:00
6:15
6:30
6:45
7:00
7:15
7:30
7:45
8:00
8:15
8:30
8:45
9:00
9:15
9:30
9:45
10:00
10:15
10:30
10:45

PACK MY BACKPACK

Are all items for school tomorrow in backpack? (✓)	

SATURDAY DATE: ________

MAKE A PLAN! 

9:00
9:30
10:00
10:30
11:00
11:30
12:00
12:30
1:00
1:30
2:00
2:30
3:00
3:30
4:00
4:30
5:00
5:30
6:00
6:30
7:00
7:30
8:00
8:30
9:00
9:30
10:00
10:30
11:00
11:30

THINGS TO WORK ON DURING THE WEEKEND 

SUNDAY DATE: ________

MAKE A PLAN! 

9:00
9:30
10:00
10:30
11:00
11:30
12:00
12:30
1:00
1:30
2:00
2:30
3:00
3:30
4:00
4:30
5:00
5:30
6:00
6:30
7:00
7:30
8:00
8:30
9:00
9:30
10:00
10:30
11:00
11:30

PACK MY BACKPACK 

Are all items for school tomorrow in backpack? (✓)	

MONDAY **DATE:** ____________________

HOMEWORK FROM SCHOOL

Classes or Activities	Due Date	In Backpack? (✓)
Other Items to take home:		

FUTURE DUE DATES AND TESTS

THINGS TO WORK ON TODAY

MAKE A PLAN!

3:00
3:15
3:30
3:45
4:00
4:15
4:30
4:45
5:00
5:15
5:30
5:45
6:00
6:15
6:30
6:45
7:00
7:15
7:30
7:45
8:00
8:15
8:30
8:45
9:00
9:15
9:30
9:45
10:00
10:15
10:30
10:45

PACK MY BACKPACK

Are all items for school tomorrow in backpack? (✓)	

TUESDAY **DATE:** ____________________ www.behaviorsciants.com

HOMEWORK FROM SCHOOL

Classes or Activities	Due Date	In Backpack? (✓)
Other Items to take home:		

FUTURE DUE DATES AND TESTS

THINGS TO WORK ON TODAY

MAKE A PLAN!

3:00
3:15
3:30
3:45
4:00
4:15
4:30
4:45
5:00
5:15
5:30
5:45
6:00
6:15
6:30
6:45
7:00
7:15
7:30
7:45
8:00
8:15
8:30
8:45
9:00
9:15
9:30
9:45
10:00
10:15
10:30
10:45

PACK MY BACKPACK

Are all items for school tomorrow in backpack? (✓)	

WEDNESDAY **DATE:** ____________________ www.behaviorsciants.com

HOMEWORK FROM SCHOOL

Classes or Activities	Due Date	In Backpack? (✓)
Other Items to take home:		

FUTURE DUE DATES AND TESTS

THINGS TO WORK ON TODAY

MAKE A PLAN!

3:00
3:15
3:30
3:45
4:00
4:15
4:30
4:45
5:00
5:15
5:30
5:45
6:00
6:15
6:30
6:45
7:00
7:15
7:30
7:45
8:00
8:15
8:30
8:45
9:00
9:15
9:30
9:45
10:00
10:15
10:30
10:45

PACK MY BACKPACK

Are all items for school tomorrow in backpack? (✓)	

THURSDAY **DATE:** ____________ www.behaviorsciants.com

HOMEWORK FROM SCHOOL

Classes or Activities	Due Date	In Backpack? (✓)
Other Items to take home:		

FUTURE DUE DATES AND TESTS

THINGS TO WORK ON TODAY

MAKE A PLAN!

3:00
3:15
3:30
3:45
4:00
4:15
4:30
4:45
5:00
5:15
5:30
5:45
6:00
6:15
6:30
6:45
7:00
7:15
7:30
7:45
8:00
8:15
8:30
8:45
9:00
9:15
9:30
9:45
10:00
10:15
10:30
10:45

PACK MY BACKPACK

Are all items for school tomorrow in backpack? (✓)	

FRIDAY **DATE:** ____________________ www.behaviorsciants.com

HOMEWORK FROM SCHOOL 

Classes or Activities	Due Date	In Backpack? (✓)
Other Items to take home:		

FUTURE DUE DATES AND TESTS

THINGS TO WORK ON TODAY

MAKE A PLAN! 

3:00	
3:15	
3:30	
3:45	
4:00	
4:15	
4:30	
4:45	
5:00	
5:15	
5:30	
5:45	
6:00	
6:15	
6:30	
6:45	
7:00	
7:15	
7:30	
7:45	
8:00	
8:15	
8:30	
8:45	
9:00	
9:15	
9:30	
9:45	
10:00	
10:15	
10:30	
10:45	

PACK MY BACKPACK

Are all items for school tomorrow in backpack? (✓)	

SATURDAY **DATE:** ____________

MAKE A PLAN!

9:00	
9:30	
10:00	
10:30	
11:00	
11:30	
12:00	
12:30	
1:00	
1:30	
2:00	
2:30	
3:00	
3:30	
4:00	
4:30	
5:00	
5:30	
6:00	
6:30	
7:00	
7:30	
8:00	
8:30	
9:00	
9:30	
10:00	
10:30	
11:00	
11:30	

THINGS TO WORK ON DURING THE WEEKEND

SUNDAY **DATE:** ____________

MAKE A PLAN!

9:00	
9:30	
10:00	
10:30	
11:00	
11:30	
12:00	
12:30	
1:00	
1:30	
2:00	
2:30	
3:00	
3:30	
4:00	
4:30	
5:00	
5:30	
6:00	
6:30	
7:00	
7:30	
8:00	
8:30	
9:00	
9:30	
10:00	
10:30	
11:00	
11:30	

PACK MY BACKPACK

Are all items for school tomorrow in backpack? (✓)	

MONDAY **DATE:** ____________ www.behaviorsciants.com

HOMEWORK FROM SCHOOL 

Classes or Activities	Due Date	In Backpack? (✓)
Other Items to take home:		

FUTURE DUE DATES AND TESTS

THINGS TO WORK ON TODAY 

MAKE A PLAN! 

3:00
3:15
3:30
3:45
4:00
4:15
4:30
4:45
5:00
5:15
5:30
5:45
6:00
6:15
6:30
6:45
7:00
7:15
7:30
7:45
8:00
8:15
8:30
8:45
9:00
9:15
9:30
9:45
10:00
10:15
10:30
10:45

PACK MY BACKPACK 

Are all items for school tomorrow in backpack? (✓)	

TUESDAY **DATE:** ____________________

HOMEWORK FROM SCHOOL

Classes or Activities	Due Date	In Backpack? (✓)
Other Items to take home:		

FUTURE DUE DATES AND TESTS

THINGS TO WORK ON TODAY

MAKE A PLAN!

3:00
3:15
3:30
3:45
4:00
4:15
4:30
4:45
5:00
5:15
5:30
5:45
6:00
6:15
6:30
6:45
7:00
7:15
7:30
7:45
8:00
8:15
8:30
8:45
9:00
9:15
9:30
9:45
10:00
10:15
10:30
10:45

PACK MY BACKPACK

Are all items for school tomorrow in backpack? (✓)	

WEDNESDAY **DATE:** ____________________ www.behaviorsciants.com

HOMEWORK FROM SCHOOL

Classes or Activities	Due Date	In Backpack? (✓)
Other Items to take home:		

FUTURE DUE DATES AND TESTS

THINGS TO WORK ON TODAY

MAKE A PLAN!

3:00
3:15
3:30
3:45
4:00
4:15
4:30
4:45
5:00
5:15
5:30
5:45
6:00
6:15
6:30
6:45
7:00
7:15
7:30
7:45
8:00
8:15
8:30
8:45
9:00
9:15
9:30
9:45
10:00
10:15
10:30
10:45

PACK MY BACKPACK

Are all items for school tomorrow in backpack? (✓)	

THURSDAY **DATE:** ____________ www.behaviorsciants.com

HOMEWORK FROM SCHOOL 

Classes or Activities	Due Date	In Backpack? (✓)
Other Items to take home:		

FUTURE DUE DATES AND TESTS 

THINGS TO WORK ON TODAY  

MAKE A PLAN!

3:00	
3:15	
3:30	
3:45	
4:00	
4:15	
4:30	
4:45	
5:00	
5:15	
5:30	
5:45	
6:00	
6:15	
6:30	
6:45	
7:00	
7:15	
7:30	
7:45	
8:00	
8:15	
8:30	
8:45	
9:00	
9:15	
9:30	
9:45	
10:00	
10:15	
10:30	
10:45	

PACK MY BACKPACK 

Are all items for school tomorrow in backpack? (✓)	

FRIDAY **DATE:** ____________ www.behaviorsciants.com

HOMEWORK FROM SCHOOL

Classes or Activities	Due Date	In Backpack? (✓)
Other Items to take home:		

FUTURE DUE DATES AND TESTS

THINGS TO WORK ON TODAY

MAKE A PLAN!

3:00
3:15
3:30
3:45
4:00
4:15
4:30
4:45
5:00
5:15
5:30
5:45
6:00
6:15
6:30
6:45
7:00
7:15
7:30
7:45
8:00
8:15
8:30
8:45
9:00
9:15
9:30
9:45
10:00
10:15
10:30
10:45

PACK MY BACKPACK

Are all items for school tomorrow in backpack? (✓)	

SATURDAY DATE: ________

MAKE A PLAN!

9:00
9:30
10:00
10:30
11:00
11:30
12:00
12:30
1:00
1:30
2:00
2:30
3:00
3:30
4:00
4:30
5:00
5:30
6:00
6:30
7:00
7:30
8:00
8:30
9:00
9:30
10:00
10:30
11:00
11:30

THINGS TO WORK ON DURING THE WEEKEND

SUNDAY DATE: ________

MAKE A PLAN!

9:00
9:30
10:00
10:30
11:00
11:30
12:00
12:30
1:00
1:30
2:00
2:30
3:00
3:30
4:00
4:30
5:00
5:30
6:00
6:30
7:00
7:30
8:00
8:30
9:00
9:30
10:00
10:30
11:00
11:30

PACK MY BACKPACK

Are all items for school tomorrow in backpack? (✓)	

MONDAY **DATE:** ____________________ www.behaviorsciants.com

HOMEWORK FROM SCHOOL

Classes or Activities	Due Date	In Backpack? (✓)
Other Items to take home:		

FUTURE DUE DATES AND TESTS

THINGS TO WORK ON TODAY

MAKE A PLAN!

3:00
3:15
3:30
3:45
4:00
4:15
4:30
4:45
5:00
5:15
5:30
5:45
6:00
6:15
6:30
6:45
7:00
7:15
7:30
7:45
8:00
8:15
8:30
8:45
9:00
9:15
9:30
9:45
10:00
10:15
10:30
10:45

PACK MY BACKPACK

Are all items for school tomorrow in backpack? (✓)	

TUESDAY **DATE:** ____________________ www.behaviorsciants.com

HOMEWORK FROM SCHOOL

Classes or Activities	Due Date	In Backpack? (✓)
Other Items to take home:		

FUTURE DUE DATES AND TESTS

THINGS TO WORK ON TODAY

MAKE A PLAN!

3:00
3:15
3:30
3:45
4:00
4:15
4:30
4:45
5:00
5:15
5:30
5:45
6:00
6:15
6:30
6:45
7:00
7:15
7:30
7:45
8:00
8:15
8:30
8:45
9:00
9:15
9:30
9:45
10:00
10:15
10:30
10:45

PACK MY BACKPACK

Are all items for school tomorrow in backpack? (✓)	

WEDNESDAY **DATE:** ____________________ www.behaviorsciants.com

HOMEWORK FROM SCHOOL

Classes or Activities	Due Date	In Backpack? (✓)
Other Items to take home:		

FUTURE DUE DATES AND TESTS

THINGS TO WORK ON TODAY

MAKE A PLAN!

3:00
3:15
3:30
3:45
4:00
4:15
4:30
4:45
5:00
5:15
5:30
5:45
6:00
6:15
6:30
6:45
7:00
7:15
7:30
7:45
8:00
8:15
8:30
8:45
9:00
9:15
9:30
9:45
10:00
10:15
10:30
10:45

PACK MY BACKPACK

Are all items for school tomorrow in backpack? (✓)	

THURSDAY **DATE:** ____________________ www.behaviorsciants.com

HOMEWORK FROM SCHOOL

Classes or Activities	Due Date	In Backpack? (✓)
Other Items to take home:		

FUTURE DUE DATES AND TESTS

THINGS TO WORK ON TODAY

MAKE A PLAN!

3:00
3:15
3:30
3:45
4:00
4:15
4:30
4:45
5:00
5:15
5:30
5:45
6:00
6:15
6:30
6:45
7:00
7:15
7:30
7:45
8:00
8:15
8:30
8:45
9:00
9:15
9:30
9:45
10:00
10:15
10:30
10:45

PACK MY BACKPACK

Are all items for school tomorrow in backpack? (✓)	

HOMEWORK FROM SCHOOL 

Classes or Activities	Due Date	In Backpack? (✓)
Other Items to take home:		

FUTURE DUE DATES AND TESTS 

THINGS TO WORK ON TODAY 

MAKE A PLAN! 

3:00
3:15
3:30
3:45
4:00
4:15
4:30
4:45
5:00
5:15
5:30
5:45
6:00
6:15
6:30
6:45
7:00
7:15
7:30
7:45
8:00
8:15
8:30
8:45
9:00
9:15
9:30
9:45
10:00
10:15
10:30
10:45

PACK MY BACKPACK 

Are all items for school tomorrow in backpack? (✓)	

SATURDAY DATE: ___________

MAKE A PLAN! 

9:00
9:30
10:00
10:30
11:00
11:30
12:00
12:30
1:00
1:30
2:00
2:30
3:00
3:30
4:00
4:30
5:00
5:30
6:00
6:30
7:00
7:30
8:00
8:30
9:00
9:30
10:00
10:30
11:00
11:30

THINGS TO WORK ON DURING THE WEEKEND 

SUNDAY DATE: ___________

MAKE A PLAN! 

9:00
9:30
10:00
10:30
11:00
11:30
12:00
12:30
1:00
1:30
2:00
2:30
3:00
3:30
4:00
4:30
5:00
5:30
6:00
6:30
7:00
7:30
8:00
8:30
9:00
9:30
10:00
10:30
11:00
11:30

PACK MY BACKPACK 

Are all items for school tomorrow in backpack? (✓)	

MONDAY **DATE:** ______________ www.behaviorsciants.com

HOMEWORK FROM SCHOOL

Classes or Activities	Due Date	In Backpack? (✓)
Other Items to take home:		

FUTURE DUE DATES AND TESTS

THINGS TO WORK ON TODAY

MAKE A PLAN!

3:00
3:15
3:30
3:45
4:00
4:15
4:30
4:45
5:00
5:15
5:30
5:45
6:00
6:15
6:30
6:45
7:00
7:15
7:30
7:45
8:00
8:15
8:30
8:45
9:00
9:15
9:30
9:45
10:00
10:15
10:30
10:45

PACK MY BACKPACK

Are all items for school tomorrow in backpack? (✓)	

TUESDAY **DATE:** ____________________ www.behaviorsciants.com

HOMEWORK FROM SCHOOL

Classes or Activities	Due Date	In Backpack? (✓)
Other Items to take home:		

FUTURE DUE DATES AND TESTS

THINGS TO WORK ON TODAY

MAKE A PLAN!

3:00

3:15

3:30

3:45

4:00

4:15

4:30

4:45

5:00

5:15

5:30

5:45

6:00

6:15

6:30

6:45

7:00

7:15

7:30

7:45

8:00

8:15

8:30

8:45

9:00

9:15

9:30

9:45

10:00

10:15

10:30

10:45

PACK MY BACKPACK

Are all items for school tomorrow in backpack? (✓)	

WEDNESDAY **DATE:** ____________________ www.behaviorsciants.com

HOMEWORK FROM SCHOOL

Classes or Activities	Due Date	In Backpack? (✓)
Other Items to take home:		

FUTURE DUE DATES AND TESTS

THINGS TO WORK ON TODAY

MAKE A PLAN!

3:00

3:15

3:30

3:45

4:00

4:15

4:30

4:45

5:00

5:15

5:30

5:45

6:00

6:15

6:30

6:45

7:00

7:15

7:30

7:45

8:00

8:15

8:30

8:45

9:00

9:15

9:30

9:45

10:00

10:15

10:30

10:45

PACK MY BACKPACK

Are all items for school tomorrow in backpack? (✓)	

THURSDAY **DATE:** ____________________

www.behaviorsciants.com

HOMEWORK FROM SCHOOL

Classes or Activities	Due Date	In Backpack? (✓)
Other Items to take home:		

FUTURE DUE DATES AND TESTS

THINGS TO WORK ON TODAY

MAKE A PLAN!

3:00
3:15
3:30
3:45
4:00
4:15
4:30
4:45
5:00
5:15
5:30
5:45
6:00
6:15
6:30
6:45
7:00
7:15
7:30
7:45
8:00
8:15
8:30
8:45
9:00
9:15
9:30
9:45
10:00
10:15
10:30
10:45

PACK MY BACKPACK

Are all items for school tomorrow in backpack? (✓)	

FRIDAY **DATE:** ____________ www.behaviorsciants.com

HOMEWORK FROM SCHOOL 

Classes or Activities	Due Date	In Backpack? (✓)
Other Items to take home:		

FUTURE DUE DATES AND TESTS 

THINGS TO WORK ON TODAY  

MAKE A PLAN! 

3:00
3:15
3:30
3:45
4:00
4:15
4:30
4:45
5:00
5:15
5:30
5:45
6:00
6:15
6:30
6:45
7:00
7:15
7:30
7:45
8:00
8:15
8:30
8:45
9:00
9:15
9:30
9:45
10:00
10:15
10:30
10:45

PACK MY BACKPACK 

Are all items for school tomorrow in backpack? (✓)	

SATURDAY DATE: ________

MAKE A PLAN! 

9:00
9:30
10:00
10:30
11:00
11:30
12:00
12:30
1:00
1:30
2:00
2:30
3:00
3:30
4:00
4:30
5:00
5:30
6:00
6:30
7:00
7:30
8:00
8:30
9:00
9:30
10:00
10:30
11:00
11:30

THINGS TO WORK ON DURING THE WEEKEND 

SUNDAY DATE: ________

MAKE A PLAN! 

9:00
9:30
10:00
10:30
11:00
11:30
12:00
12:30
1:00
1:30
2:00
2:30
3:00
3:30
4:00
4:30
5:00
5:30
6:00
6:30
7:00
7:30
8:00
8:30
9:00
9:30
10:00
10:30
11:00
11:30

PACK MY BACKPACK 

Are all items for school tomorrow in backpack? (✓)	

MONDAY **DATE:** ____________________ www.behaviorsciants.com

HOMEWORK FROM SCHOOL

Classes or Activities	Due Date	In Backpack? (✓)
Other Items to take home:		

FUTURE DUE DATES AND TESTS

THINGS TO WORK ON TODAY

MAKE A PLAN!

3:00
3:15
3:30
3:45
4:00
4:15
4:30
4:45
5:00
5:15
5:30
5:45
6:00
6:15
6:30
6:45
7:00
7:15
7:30
7:45
8:00
8:15
8:30
8:45
9:00
9:15
9:30
9:45
10:00
10:15
10:30
10:45

PACK MY BACKPACK

Are all items for school tomorrow in backpack? (✓)	

TUESDAY **DATE:** ______________ www.behaviorsciants.com

HOMEWORK FROM SCHOOL 

Classes or Activities	Due Date	In Backpack? (✓)
Other Items to take home:		

FUTURE DUE DATES AND TESTS 

THINGS TO WORK ON TODAY  

MAKE A PLAN! 

3:00
3:15
3:30
3:45
4:00
4:15
4:30
4:45
5:00
5:15
5:30
5:45
6:00
6:15
6:30
6:45
7:00
7:15
7:30
7:45
8:00
8:15
8:30
8:45
9:00
9:15
9:30
9:45
10:00
10:15
10:30
10:45

PACK MY BACKPACK 

Are all items for school tomorrow in backpack? (✓)	

WEDNESDAY **DATE:** ____________ www.behaviorsciants.com

HOMEWORK FROM SCHOOL

Classes or Activities	Due Date	In Backpack? (✓)
Other Items to take home:		

FUTURE DUE DATES AND TESTS

THINGS TO WORK ON TODAY

MAKE A PLAN!

3:00
3:15
3:30
3:45
4:00
4:15
4:30
4:45
5:00
5:15
5:30
5:45
6:00
6:15
6:30
6:45
7:00
7:15
7:30
7:45
8:00
8:15
8:30
8:45
9:00
9:15
9:30
9:45
10:00
10:15
10:30
10:45

PACK MY BACKPACK

Are all items for school tomorrow in backpack? (✓)	

THURSDAY **DATE:** ______________ www.behaviorsciants.com

HOMEWORK FROM SCHOOL

Classes or Activities	Due Date	In Backpack? (✓)
Other Items to take home:		

FUTURE DUE DATES AND TESTS

THINGS TO WORK ON TODAY

MAKE A PLAN!

3:00
3:15
3:30
3:45
4:00
4:15
4:30
4:45
5:00
5:15
5:30
5:45
6:00
6:15
6:30
6:45
7:00
7:15
7:30
7:45
8:00
8:15
8:30
8:45
9:00
9:15
9:30
9:45
10:00
10:15
10:30
10:45

PACK MY BACKPACK

Are all items for school tomorrow in backpack? (✓)	

FRIDAY DATE: ____________________ www.behaviorsciants.com

HOMEWORK FROM SCHOOL

Classes or Activities	Due Date	In Backpack? (✓)
Other Items to take home:		

FUTURE DUE DATES AND TESTS

THINGS TO WORK ON TODAY

MAKE A PLAN!

3:00
3:15
3:30
3:45
4:00
4:15
4:30
4:45
5:00
5:15
5:30
5:45
6:00
6:15
6:30
6:45
7:00
7:15
7:30
7:45
8:00
8:15
8:30
8:45
9:00
9:15
9:30
9:45
10:00
10:15
10:30
10:45

PACK MY BACKPACK

Are all items for school tomorrow in backpack? (✓)	

SATURDAY DATE: ________

MAKE A PLAN!

9:00
9:30
10:00
10:30
11:00
11:30
12:00
12:30
1:00
1:30
2:00
2:30
3:00
3:30
4:00
4:30
5:00
5:30
6:00
6:30
7:00
7:30
8:00
8:30
9:00
9:30
10:00
10:30
11:00
11:30

THINGS TO WORK ON DURING THE WEEKEND

SUNDAY DATE: ________

MAKE A PLAN!

9:00
9:30
10:00
10:30
11:00
11:30
12:00
12:30
1:00
1:30
2:00
2:30
3:00
3:30
4:00
4:30
5:00
5:30
6:00
6:30
7:00
7:30
8:00
8:30
9:00
9:30
10:00
10:30
11:00
11:30

PACK MY BACKPACK

Are all items for school tomorrow in backpack? (✓)	

MONDAY **DATE:** ____________________ www.behaviorsciants.com

HOMEWORK FROM SCHOOL 

Classes or Activities	Due Date	In Backpack? (✓)
Other Items to take home:		

FUTURE DUE DATES AND TESTS 

THINGS TO WORK ON TODAY 

MAKE A PLAN! 

3:00
3:15
3:30
3:45
4:00
4:15
4:30
4:45
5:00
5:15
5:30
5:45
6:00
6:15
6:30
6:45
7:00
7:15
7:30
7:45
8:00
8:15
8:30
8:45
9:00
9:15
9:30
9:45
10:00
10:15
10:30
10:45

PACK MY BACKPACK 

Are all items for school tomorrow in backpack? (✓)	

TUESDAY **DATE:** ____________________ www.behaviorsciants.com

HOMEWORK FROM SCHOOL

Classes or Activities	Due Date	In Backpack? (✓)
Other Items to take home:		

FUTURE DUE DATES AND TESTS

THINGS TO WORK ON TODAY

MAKE A PLAN!

3:00

3:15

3:30

3:45

4:00

4:15

4:30

4:45

5:00

5:15

5:30

5:45

6:00

6:15

6:30

6:45

7:00

7:15

7:30

7:45

8:00

8:15

8:30

8:45

9:00

9:15

9:30

9:45

10:00

10:15

10:30

10:45

PACK MY BACKPACK

Are all items for school tomorrow in backpack? (✓)	

WEDNESDAY **DATE:** ____________ www.behaviorsciants.com

HOMEWORK FROM SCHOOL

Classes or Activities	Due Date	In Backpack? (✓)
Other Items to take home:		

FUTURE DUE DATES AND TESTS

THINGS TO WORK ON TODAY

MAKE A PLAN!

3:00
3:15
3:30
3:45
4:00
4:15
4:30
4:45
5:00
5:15
5:30
5:45
6:00
6:15
6:30
6:45
7:00
7:15
7:30
7:45
8:00
8:15
8:30
8:45
9:00
9:15
9:30
9:45
10:00
10:15
10:30
10:45

PACK MY BACKPACK

Are all items for school tomorrow in backpack? (✓)	

THURSDAY **DATE:** ____________ www.behaviorsciants.com

HOMEWORK FROM SCHOOL 

Classes or Activities	Due Date	In Backpack? (✓)
Other Items to take home:		

FUTURE DUE DATES AND TESTS 

THINGS TO WORK ON TODAY  

MAKE A PLAN!

3:00
3:15
3:30
3:45
4:00
4:15
4:30
4:45
5:00
5:15
5:30
5:45
6:00
6:15
6:30
6:45
7:00
7:15
7:30
7:45
8:00
8:15
8:30
8:45
9:00
9:15
9:30
9:45
10:00
10:15
10:30
10:45

PACK MY BACKPACK 

Are all items for school tomorrow in backpack? (✓)	

FRIDAY **DATE:** ____________________ www.behaviorsciants.com

HOMEWORK FROM SCHOOL

Classes or Activities	Due Date	In Backpack? (✓)
Other Items to take home:		

FUTURE DUE DATES AND TESTS

THINGS TO WORK ON TODAY

MAKE A PLAN!

3:00
3:15
3:30
3:45
4:00
4:15
4:30
4:45
5:00
5:15
5:30
5:45
6:00
6:15
6:30
6:45
7:00
7:15
7:30
7:45
8:00
8:15
8:30
8:45
9:00
9:15
9:30
9:45
10:00
10:15
10:30
10:45

PACK MY BACKPACK

Are all items for school tomorrow in backpack? (✓)	

SATURDAY DATE: ___________

MAKE A PLAN! 

9:00
9:30
10:00
10:30
11:00
11:30
12:00
12:30
1:00
1:30
2:00
2:30
3:00
3:30
4:00
4:30
5:00
5:30
6:00
6:30
7:00
7:30
8:00
8:30
9:00
9:30
10:00
10:30
11:00
11:30

THINGS TO WORK ON DURING THE WEEKEND 

SUNDAY DATE: ___________

MAKE A PLAN! 

9:00
9:30
10:00
10:30
11:00
11:30
12:00
12:30
1:00
1:30
2:00
2:30
3:00
3:30
4:00
4:30
5:00
5:30
6:00
6:30
7:00
7:30
8:00
8:30
9:00
9:30
10:00
10:30
11:00
11:30

PACK MY BACKPACK 

Are all items for school tomorrow in backpack? (✓)	

MONDAY **DATE:** ____________________ www.behaviorsciants.com

HOMEWORK FROM SCHOOL

Classes or Activities	Due Date	In Backpack? (✓)
Other Items to take home:		

FUTURE DUE DATES AND TESTS

THINGS TO WORK ON TODAY

MAKE A PLAN!

3:00
3:15
3:30
3:45
4:00
4:15
4:30
4:45
5:00
5:15
5:30
5:45
6:00
6:15
6:30
6:45
7:00
7:15
7:30
7:45
8:00
8:15
8:30
8:45
9:00
9:15
9:30
9:45
10:00
10:15
10:30
10:45

PACK MY BACKPACK

Are all items for school tomorrow in backpack? (✓)	

TUESDAY **DATE:** ____________________ www.behaviorsciants.com

HOMEWORK FROM SCHOOL 

Classes or Activities	Due Date	In Backpack? (✓)
Other Items to take home:		

FUTURE DUE DATES AND TESTS

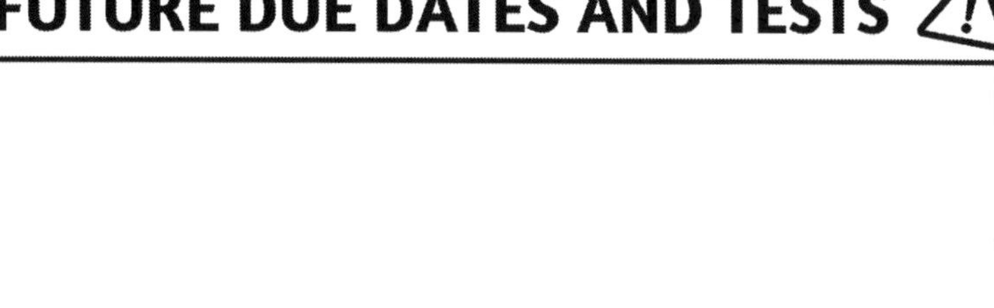

THINGS TO WORK ON TODAY 

MAKE A PLAN! 

3:00
3:15
3:30
3:45
4:00
4:15
4:30
4:45
5:00
5:15
5:30
5:45
6:00
6:15
6:30
6:45
7:00
7:15
7:30
7:45
8:00
8:15
8:30
8:45
9:00
9:15
9:30
9:45
10:00
10:15
10:30
10:45

PACK MY BACKPACK 

Are all items for school tomorrow in backpack? (✓)	

WEDNESDAY **DATE:** ____________________ www.behaviorsciants.com

HOMEWORK FROM SCHOOL

Classes or Activities	Due Date	In Backpack? (✓)
Other Items to take home:		

FUTURE DUE DATES AND TESTS

THINGS TO WORK ON TODAY

MAKE A PLAN!

3:00
3:15
3:30
3:45
4:00
4:15
4:30
4:45
5:00
5:15
5:30
5:45
6:00
6:15
6:30
6:45
7:00
7:15
7:30
7:45
8:00
8:15
8:30
8:45
9:00
9:15
9:30
9:45
10:00
10:15
10:30
10:45

PACK MY BACKPACK

Are all items for school tomorrow in backpack? (✓)	

THURSDAY **DATE:** ____________ www.behaviorsciants.com

HOMEWORK FROM SCHOOL

Classes or Activities	Due Date	In Backpack? (✓)
Other Items to take home:		

FUTURE DUE DATES AND TESTS

THINGS TO WORK ON TODAY

MAKE A PLAN!

3:00
3:15
3:30
3:45
4:00
4:15
4:30
4:45
5:00
5:15
5:30
5:45
6:00
6:15
6:30
6:45
7:00
7:15
7:30
7:45
8:00
8:15
8:30
8:45
9:00
9:15
9:30
9:45
10:00
10:15
10:30
10:45

PACK MY BACKPACK

Are all items for school tomorrow in backpack? (✓)	

FRIDAY **DATE:** ____________ www.behaviorsciants.com

HOMEWORK FROM SCHOOL

Classes or Activities	Due Date	In Backpack? (✓)
Other Items to take home:		

FUTURE DUE DATES AND TESTS

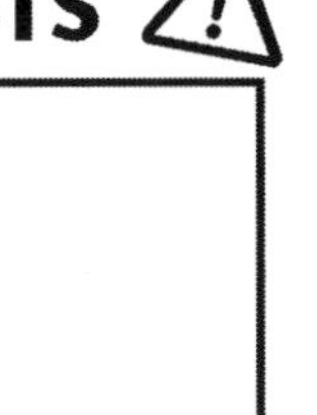

THINGS TO WORK ON TODAY

MAKE A PLAN!

3:00
3:15
3:30
3:45
4:00
4:15
4:30
4:45
5:00
5:15
5:30
5:45
6:00
6:15
6:30
6:45
7:00
7:15
7:30
7:45
8:00
8:15
8:30
8:45
9:00
9:15
9:30
9:45
10:00
10:15
10:30
10:45

PACK MY BACKPACK

Are all items for school tomorrow in backpack? (✓)	

SATURDAY DATE: ________

MAKE A PLAN!

9:00

9:30

10:00

10:30

11:00

11:30

12:00

12:30

1:00

1:30

2:00

2:30

3:00

3:30

4:00

4:30

5:00

5:30

6:00

6:30

7:00

7:30

8:00

8:30

9:00

9:30

10:00

10:30

11:00

11:30

THINGS TO WORK ON DURING THE WEEKEND

SUNDAY DATE: ________

MAKE A PLAN!

9:00

9:30

10:00

10:30

11:00

11:30

12:00

12:30

1:00

1:30

2:00

2:30

3:00

3:30

4:00

4:30

5:00

5:30

6:00

6:30

7:00

7:30

8:00

8:30

9:00

9:30

10:00

10:30

11:00

11:30

PACK MY BACKPACK

Are all items for school tomorrow in backpack? (✓)	

MONDAY **DATE:** ____________ www.behaviorsciants.com

HOMEWORK FROM SCHOOL 

Classes or Activities	Due Date	In Backpack? (✓)
Other Items to take home:		

FUTURE DUE DATES AND TESTS 

THINGS TO WORK ON TODAY  

MAKE A PLAN! 

3:00
3:15
3:30
3:45
4:00
4:15
4:30
4:45
5:00
5:15
5:30
5:45
6:00
6:15
6:30
6:45
7:00
7:15
7:30
7:45
8:00
8:15
8:30
8:45
9:00
9:15
9:30
9:45
10:00
10:15
10:30
10:45

PACK MY BACKPACK 

Are all items for school tomorrow in backpack? (✓)	

TUESDAY **DATE:** ____________________ www.behaviorsciants.com

HOMEWORK FROM SCHOOL 

Classes or Activities	Due Date	In Backpack? (✓)
Other Items to take home:		

FUTURE DUE DATES AND TESTS 

THINGS TO WORK ON TODAY  

MAKE A PLAN!

3:00	
3:15	
3:30	
3:45	
4:00	
4:15	
4:30	
4:45	
5:00	
5:15	
5:30	
5:45	
6:00	
6:15	
6:30	
6:45	
7:00	
7:15	
7:30	
7:45	
8:00	
8:15	
8:30	
8:45	
9:00	
9:15	
9:30	
9:45	
10:00	
10:15	
10:30	
10:45	

PACK MY BACKPACK 

Are all items for school tomorrow in backpack? (✓)	

WEDNESDAY **DATE:** ______________ www.behaviorsciants.com

HOMEWORK FROM SCHOOL

Classes or Activities	Due Date	In Backpack? (✓)
Other Items to take home:		

FUTURE DUE DATES AND TESTS

THINGS TO WORK ON TODAY

MAKE A PLAN!

3:00
3:15
3:30
3:45
4:00
4:15
4:30
4:45
5:00
5:15
5:30
5:45
6:00
6:15
6:30
6:45
7:00
7:15
7:30
7:45
8:00
8:15
8:30
8:45
9:00
9:15
9:30
9:45
10:00
10:15
10:30
10:45

PACK MY BACKPACK

Are all items for school tomorrow in backpack? (✓)	

THURSDAY **DATE:** ____________ www.behaviorsciants.com

HOMEWORK FROM SCHOOL 

Classes or Activities	Due Date	In Backpack? (✓)
Other Items to take home:		

FUTURE DUE DATES AND TESTS 

THINGS TO WORK ON TODAY  

MAKE A PLAN! 

3:00
3:15
3:30
3:45
4:00
4:15
4:30
4:45
5:00
5:15
5:30
5:45
6:00
6:15
6:30
6:45
7:00
7:15
7:30
7:45
8:00
8:15
8:30
8:45
9:00
9:15
9:30
9:45
10:00
10:15
10:30
10:45

PACK MY BACKPACK 

Are all items for school tomorrow in backpack? (✓)	

FRIDAY **DATE:** ____________ www.behaviorsciants.com

HOMEWORK FROM SCHOOL

Classes or Activities	Due Date	In Backpack? (✓)
Other Items to take home:		

FUTURE DUE DATES AND TESTS

THINGS TO WORK ON TODAY

MAKE A PLAN!

3:00
3:15
3:30
3:45
4:00
4:15
4:30
4:45
5:00
5:15
5:30
5:45
6:00
6:15
6:30
6:45
7:00
7:15
7:30
7:45
8:00
8:15
8:30
8:45
9:00
9:15
9:30
9:45
10:00
10:15
10:30
10:45

PACK MY BACKPACK

Are all items for school tomorrow in backpack? (✓)	

SATURDAY DATE: ________

MAKE A PLAN! 

9:00
9:30
10:00
10:30
11:00
11:30
12:00
12:30
1:00
1:30
2:00
2:30
3:00
3:30
4:00
4:30
5:00
5:30
6:00
6:30
7:00
7:30
8:00
8:30
9:00
9:30
10:00
10:30
11:00
11:30

THINGS TO WORK ON DURING THE WEEKEND 

SUNDAY DATE: ________

MAKE A PLAN! 

9:00
9:30
10:00
10:30
11:00
11:30
12:00
12:30
1:00
1:30
2:00
2:30
3:00
3:30
4:00
4:30
5:00
5:30
6:00
6:30
7:00
7:30
8:00
8:30
9:00
9:30
10:00
10:30
11:00
11:30

PACK MY BACKPACK 

Are all items for school tomorrow in backpack? (✓)	

MONDAY **DATE:** ____________________ www.behaviorsciants.com

HOMEWORK FROM SCHOOL 

Classes or Activities	Due Date	In Backpack? (✓)
Other Items to take home:		

FUTURE DUE DATES AND TESTS 

THINGS TO WORK ON TODAY  

MAKE A PLAN! 

3:00
3:15
3:30
3:45
4:00
4:15
4:30
4:45
5:00
5:15
5:30
5:45
6:00
6:15
6:30
6:45
7:00
7:15
7:30
7:45
8:00
8:15
8:30
8:45
9:00
9:15
9:30
9:45
10:00
10:15
10:30
10:45

PACK MY BACKPACK 

Are all items for school tomorrow in backpack? (✓)	

TUESDAY **DATE:** ____________________ www.behaviorsciants.com

HOMEWORK FROM SCHOOL

Classes or Activities	Due Date	In Backpack? (✓)
Other Items to take home:		

FUTURE DUE DATES AND TESTS

THINGS TO WORK ON TODAY

MAKE A PLAN!

3:00
3:15
3:30
3:45
4:00
4:15
4:30
4:45
5:00
5:15
5:30
5:45
6:00
6:15
6:30
6:45
7:00
7:15
7:30
7:45
8:00
8:15
8:30
8:45
9:00
9:15
9:30
9:45
10:00
10:15
10:30
10:45

PACK MY BACKPACK

Are all items for school tomorrow in backpack? (✓)	

WEDNESDAY **DATE:** ____________________ www.behaviorsciants.com

HOMEWORK FROM SCHOOL

Classes or Activities	Due Date	In Backpack? (✓)
Other Items to take home:		

FUTURE DUE DATES AND TESTS

THINGS TO WORK ON TODAY

MAKE A PLAN!

3:00	
3:15	
3:30	
3:45	
4:00	
4:15	
4:30	
4:45	
5:00	
5:15	
5:30	
5:45	
6:00	
6:15	
6:30	
6:45	
7:00	
7:15	
7:30	
7:45	
8:00	
8:15	
8:30	
8:45	
9:00	
9:15	
9:30	
9:45	
10:00	
10:15	
10:30	
10:45	

PACK MY BACKPACK

Are all items for school tomorrow in backpack? (✓)	

THURSDAY **DATE:** ____________ www.behaviorsciants.com

HOMEWORK FROM SCHOOL

Classes or Activities	Due Date	In Backpack? (✓)
Other Items to take home:		

FUTURE DUE DATES AND TESTS

THINGS TO WORK ON TODAY

MAKE A PLAN!

3:00

3:15

3:30

3:45

4:00

4:15

4:30

4:45

5:00

5:15

5:30

5:45

6:00

6:15

6:30

6:45

7:00

7:15

7:30

7:45

8:00

8:15

8:30

8:45

9:00

9:15

9:30

9:45

10:00

10:15

10:30

10:45

PACK MY BACKPACK

Are all items for school tomorrow in backpack? (✓)	

FRIDAY **DATE:** ____________ www.behaviorsciants.com

HOMEWORK FROM SCHOOL

Classes or Activities	Due Date	In Backpack? (✓)
Other Items to take home:		

FUTURE DUE DATES AND TESTS

THINGS TO WORK ON TODAY

MAKE A PLAN!

3:00
3:15
3:30
3:45
4:00
4:15
4:30
4:45
5:00
5:15
5:30
5:45
6:00
6:15
6:30
6:45
7:00
7:15
7:30
7:45
8:00
8:15
8:30
8:45
9:00
9:15
9:30
9:45
10:00
10:15
10:30
10:45

PACK MY BACKPACK

Are all items for school tomorrow in backpack? (✓)	

SATURDAY DATE: ________

MAKE A PLAN! 

9:00
9:30
10:00
10:30
11:00
11:30
12:00
12:30
1:00
1:30
2:00
2:30
3:00
3:30
4:00
4:30
5:00
5:30
6:00
6:30
7:00
7:30
8:00
8:30
9:00
9:30
10:00
10:30
11:00
11:30

THINGS TO WORK ON DURING THE WEEKEND 

SUNDAY DATE: ________

MAKE A PLAN! 

9:00
9:30
10:00
10:30
11:00
11:30
12:00
12:30
1:00
1:30
2:00
2:30
3:00
3:30
4:00
4:30
5:00
5:30
6:00
6:30
7:00
7:30
8:00
8:30
9:00
9:30
10:00
10:30
11:00
11:30

PACK MY BACKPACK 

Are all items for school tomorrow in backpack? (✓)	

MONDAY DATE: ____________________ www.behaviorsciants.com

HOMEWORK FROM SCHOOL

Classes or Activities	Due Date	In Backpack? (✓)
Other Items to take home:		

FUTURE DUE DATES AND TESTS

THINGS TO WORK ON TODAY

MAKE A PLAN!

3:00

3:15

3:30

3:45

4:00

4:15

4:30

4:45

5:00

5:15

5:30

5:45

6:00

6:15

6:30

6:45

7:00

7:15

7:30

7:45

8:00

8:15

8:30

8:45

9:00

9:15

9:30

9:45

10:00

10:15

10:30

10:45

PACK MY BACKPACK

Are all items for school tomorrow in backpack? (✓)	

TUESDAY **DATE:** ____________ www.behaviorsciants.com

HOMEWORK FROM SCHOOL

Classes or Activities	Due Date	In Backpack? (✓)
Other Items to take home:		

FUTURE DUE DATES AND TESTS

THINGS TO WORK ON TODAY

MAKE A PLAN!

3:00
3:15
3:30
3:45
4:00
4:15
4:30
4:45
5:00
5:15
5:30
5:45
6:00
6:15
6:30
6:45
7:00
7:15
7:30
7:45
8:00
8:15
8:30
8:45
9:00
9:15
9:30
9:45
10:00
10:15
10:30
10:45

PACK MY BACKPACK

Are all items for school tomorrow in backpack? (✓)	

WEDNESDAY **DATE:** ____________________ www.behaviorsciants.com

HOMEWORK FROM SCHOOL

Classes or Activities	Due Date	In Backpack? (✓)
Other Items to take home:		

FUTURE DUE DATES AND TESTS

THINGS TO WORK ON TODAY

MAKE A PLAN!

3:00
3:15
3:30
3:45
4:00
4:15
4:30
4:45
5:00
5:15
5:30
5:45
6:00
6:15
6:30
6:45
7:00
7:15
7:30
7:45
8:00
8:15
8:30
8:45
9:00
9:15
9:30
9:45
10:00
10:15
10:30
10:45

PACK MY BACKPACK

Are all items for school tomorrow in backpack? (✓)	

THURSDAY **DATE:** ____________________ www.behaviorsciants.com

HOMEWORK FROM SCHOOL

Classes or Activities	Due Date	In Backpack? (✓)
Other Items to take home:		

FUTURE DUE DATES AND TESTS

THINGS TO WORK ON TODAY

MAKE A PLAN!

3:00
3:15
3:30
3:45
4:00
4:15
4:30
4:45
5:00
5:15
5:30
5:45
6:00
6:15
6:30
6:45
7:00
7:15
7:30
7:45
8:00
8:15
8:30
8:45
9:00
9:15
9:30
9:45
10:00
10:15
10:30
10:45

PACK MY BACKPACK

Are all items for school tomorrow in backpack? (✓)	

FRIDAY **DATE:** ____________ www.behaviorsciants.com

HOMEWORK FROM SCHOOL

Classes or Activities	Due Date	In Backpack? (✓)
Other Items to take home:		

FUTURE DUE DATES AND TESTS

THINGS TO WORK ON TODAY

MAKE A PLAN!

3:00
3:15
3:30
3:45
4:00
4:15
4:30
4:45
5:00
5:15
5:30
5:45
6:00
6:15
6:30
6:45
7:00
7:15
7:30
7:45
8:00
8:15
8:30
8:45
9:00
9:15
9:30
9:45
10:00
10:15
10:30
10:45

PACK MY BACKPACK

Are all items for school tomorrow in backpack? (✓)	

SATURDAY DATE: ______

MAKE A PLAN!

9:00
9:30
10:00
10:30
11:00
11:30
12:00
12:30
1:00
1:30
2:00
2:30
3:00
3:30
4:00
4:30
5:00
5:30
6:00
6:30
7:00
7:30
8:00
8:30
9:00
9:30
10:00
10:30
11:00
11:30

THINGS TO WORK ON DURING THE WEEKEND

SUNDAY DATE: ______

MAKE A PLAN!

9:00
9:30
10:00
10:30
11:00
11:30
12:00
12:30
1:00
1:30
2:00
2:30
3:00
3:30
4:00
4:30
5:00
5:30
6:00
6:30
7:00
7:30
8:00
8:30
9:00
9:30
10:00
10:30
11:00
11:30

PACK MY BACKPACK

Are all items for school tomorrow in backpack? (✓)	

MONDAY **DATE:** ______________________ www.behaviorsciants.com

HOMEWORK FROM SCHOOL

Classes or Activities	Due Date	In Backpack? (✓)
Other Items to take home:		

FUTURE DUE DATES AND TESTS

THINGS TO WORK ON TODAY

MAKE A PLAN!

3:00
3:15
3:30
3:45
4:00
4:15
4:30
4:45
5:00
5:15
5:30
5:45
6:00
6:15
6:30
6:45
7:00
7:15
7:30
7:45
8:00
8:15
8:30
8:45
9:00
9:15
9:30
9:45
10:00
10:15
10:30
10:45

PACK MY BACKPACK

Are all items for school tomorrow in backpack? (✓)	

TUESDAY **DATE:** ____________________ www.behaviorsciants.com

HOMEWORK FROM SCHOOL 

Classes or Activities	Due Date	In Backpack? (✓)
Other Items to take home:		

FUTURE DUE DATES AND TESTS 

THINGS TO WORK ON TODAY  

MAKE A PLAN!

3:00
3:15
3:30
3:45
4:00
4:15
4:30
4:45
5:00
5:15
5:30
5:45
6:00
6:15
6:30
6:45
7:00
7:15
7:30
7:45
8:00
8:15
8:30
8:45
9:00
9:15
9:30
9:45
10:00
10:15
10:30
10:45

PACK MY BACKPACK 

Are all items for school tomorrow in backpack? (✓)	

WEDNESDAY **DATE:** ____________________ www.behaviorsciants.com

HOMEWORK FROM SCHOOL 

Classes or Activities	Due Date	In Backpack? (✓)
Other Items to take home:		

FUTURE DUE DATES AND TESTS 

THINGS TO WORK ON TODAY  

MAKE A PLAN!

3:00
3:15
3:30
3:45
4:00
4:15
4:30
4:45
5:00
5:15
5:30
5:45
6:00
6:15
6:30
6:45
7:00
7:15
7:30
7:45
8:00
8:15
8:30
8:45
9:00
9:15
9:30
9:45
10:00
10:15
10:30
10:45

PACK MY BACKPACK 

Are all items for school tomorrow in backpack? (✓)	

THURSDAY **DATE:** ____________________ www.behaviorsciants.com

HOMEWORK FROM SCHOOL 

Classes or Activities	Due Date	In Backpack? (✓)
Other Items to take home:		

FUTURE DUE DATES AND TESTS 

THINGS TO WORK ON TODAY  

MAKE A PLAN!

3:00
3:15
3:30
3:45
4:00
4:15
4:30
4:45
5:00
5:15
5:30
5:45
6:00
6:15
6:30
6:45
7:00
7:15
7:30
7:45
8:00
8:15
8:30
8:45
9:00
9:15
9:30
9:45
10:00
10:15
10:30
10:45

PACK MY BACKPACK 

Are all items for school tomorrow in backpack? (✓)	

FRIDAY **DATE:** ____________ www.behaviorsciants.com

HOMEWORK FROM SCHOOL 

Classes or Activities	Due Date	In Backpack? (✓)
Other Items to take home:		

FUTURE DUE DATES AND TESTS 

THINGS TO WORK ON TODAY 

MAKE A PLAN! 

3:00
3:15
3:30
3:45
4:00
4:15
4:30
4:45
5:00
5:15
5:30
5:45
6:00
6:15
6:30
6:45
7:00
7:15
7:30
7:45
8:00
8:15
8:30
8:45
9:00
9:15
9:30
9:45
10:00
10:15
10:30
10:45

PACK MY BACKPACK 

Are all items for school tomorrow in backpack? (✓)	

SATURDAY DATE: ____________

MAKE A PLAN!

9:00

9:30

10:00

10:30

11:00

11:30

12:00

12:30

1:00

1:30

2:00

2:30

3:00

3:30

4:00

4:30

5:00

5:30

6:00

6:30

7:00

7:30

8:00

8:30

9:00

9:30

10:00

10:30

11:00

11:30

THINGS TO WORK ON DURING THE WEEKEND

SUNDAY DATE: ____________

MAKE A PLAN!

9:00

9:30

10:00

10:30

11:00

11:30

12:00

12:30

1:00

1:30

2:00

2:30

3:00

3:30

4:00

4:30

5:00

5:30

6:00

6:30

7:00

7:30

8:00

8:30

9:00

9:30

10:00

10:30

11:00

11:30

PACK MY BACKPACK

Are all items for school tomorrow in backpack? (✓)	

MONDAY **DATE:** ____________

HOMEWORK FROM SCHOOL

Classes or Activities	Due Date	In Backpack? (✓)
Other Items to take home:		

FUTURE DUE DATES AND TESTS

THINGS TO WORK ON TODAY

MAKE A PLAN!

3:00
3:15
3:30
3:45
4:00
4:15
4:30
4:45
5:00
5:15
5:30
5:45
6:00
6:15
6:30
6:45
7:00
7:15
7:30
7:45
8:00
8:15
8:30
8:45
9:00
9:15
9:30
9:45
10:00
10:15
10:30
10:45

PACK MY BACKPACK

Are all items for school tomorrow in backpack? (✓)	

TUESDAY **DATE:** ____________________ www.behaviorsciants.com

HOMEWORK FROM SCHOOL

Classes or Activities	Due Date	In Backpack? (✓)
Other Items to take home:		

FUTURE DUE DATES AND TESTS

THINGS TO WORK ON TODAY

MAKE A PLAN!

3:00
3:15
3:30
3:45
4:00
4:15
4:30
4:45
5:00
5:15
5:30
5:45
6:00
6:15
6:30
6:45
7:00
7:15
7:30
7:45
8:00
8:15
8:30
8:45
9:00
9:15
9:30
9:45
10:00
10:15
10:30
10:45

PACK MY BACKPACK

Are all items for school tomorrow in backpack? (✓)	

WEDNESDAY **DATE:** ______________ www.behaviorsciants.com

HOMEWORK FROM SCHOOL

Classes or Activities	Due Date	In Backpack? (✓)
Other Items to take home:		

FUTURE DUE DATES AND TESTS

THINGS TO WORK ON TODAY

MAKE A PLAN!

3:00
3:15
3:30
3:45
4:00
4:15
4:30
4:45
5:00
5:15
5:30
5:45
6:00
6:15
6:30
6:45
7:00
7:15
7:30
7:45
8:00
8:15
8:30
8:45
9:00
9:15
9:30
9:45
10:00
10:15
10:30
10:45

PACK MY BACKPACK

Are all items for school tomorrow in backpack? (✓)	

THURSDAY **DATE:** ____________________ www.behaviorsciants.com

HOMEWORK FROM SCHOOL

Classes or Activities	Due Date	In Backpack? (✓)
Other Items to take home:		

FUTURE DUE DATES AND TESTS

THINGS TO WORK ON TODAY

MAKE A PLAN!

3:00
3:15
3:30
3:45
4:00
4:15
4:30
4:45
5:00
5:15
5:30
5:45
6:00
6:15
6:30
6:45
7:00
7:15
7:30
7:45
8:00
8:15
8:30
8:45
9:00
9:15
9:30
9:45
10:00
10:15
10:30
10:45

PACK MY BACKPACK

Are all items for school tomorrow in backpack? (✓)	

FRIDAY **DATE:** ____________________ www.behaviorsciants.com

HOMEWORK FROM SCHOOL

Classes or Activities	Due Date	In Backpack? (✓)
Other Items to take home:		

FUTURE DUE DATES AND TESTS

THINGS TO WORK ON TODAY

MAKE A PLAN!

3:00
3:15
3:30
3:45
4:00
4:15
4:30
4:45
5:00
5:15
5:30
5:45
6:00
6:15
6:30
6:45
7:00
7:15
7:30
7:45
8:00
8:15
8:30
8:45
9:00
9:15
9:30
9:45
10:00
10:15
10:30
10:45

PACK MY BACKPACK

Are all items for school tomorrow in backpack? (✓)	

SATURDAY DATE: ____________

MAKE A PLAN! 

9:00
9:30
10:00
10:30
11:00
11:30
12:00
12:30
1:00
1:30
2:00
2:30
3:00
3:30
4:00
4:30
5:00
5:30
6:00
6:30
7:00
7:30
8:00
8:30
9:00
9:30
10:00
10:30
11:00
11:30

THINGS TO WORK ON DURING THE WEEKEND 

SUNDAY DATE: ____________

MAKE A PLAN! 

9:00
9:30
10:00
10:30
11:00
11:30
12:00
12:30
1:00
1:30
2:00
2:30
3:00
3:30
4:00
4:30
5:00
5:30
6:00
6:30
7:00
7:30
8:00
8:30
9:00
9:30
10:00
10:30
11:00
11:30

PACK MY BACKPACK 

Are all items for school tomorrow in backpack? (✓)	

MONDAY **DATE:** ____________________ www.behaviorsciants.com

HOMEWORK FROM SCHOOL

Classes or Activities	Due Date	In Backpack? (✓)
Other Items to take home:		

FUTURE DUE DATES AND TESTS

THINGS TO WORK ON TODAY

MAKE A PLAN!

3:00
3:15
3:30
3:45
4:00
4:15
4:30
4:45
5:00
5:15
5:30
5:45
6:00
6:15
6:30
6:45
7:00
7:15
7:30
7:45
8:00
8:15
8:30
8:45
9:00
9:15
9:30
9:45
10:00
10:15
10:30
10:45

PACK MY BACKPACK

Are all items for school tomorrow in backpack? (✓)	

TUESDAY **DATE:** ____________________ www.behaviorsciants.com

HOMEWORK FROM SCHOOL

Classes or Activities	Due Date	In Backpack? (✓)

Other Items to take home:	

FUTURE DUE DATES AND TESTS

THINGS TO WORK ON TODAY

MAKE A PLAN!

3:00
3:15
3:30
3:45
4:00
4:15
4:30
4:45
5:00
5:15
5:30
5:45
6:00
6:15
6:30
6:45
7:00
7:15
7:30
7:45
8:00
8:15
8:30
8:45
9:00
9:15
9:30
9:45
10:00
10:15
10:30
10:45

PACK MY BACKPACK

Are all items for school tomorrow in backpack? (✓)	

WEDNESDAY **DATE:** ____________ www.behaviorsciants.com

HOMEWORK FROM SCHOOL

Classes or Activities	Due Date	In Backpack? (✓)
Other Items to take home:		

FUTURE DUE DATES AND TESTS

THINGS TO WORK ON TODAY

MAKE A PLAN!

3:00
3:15
3:30
3:45
4:00
4:15
4:30
4:45
5:00
5:15
5:30
5:45
6:00
6:15
6:30
6:45
7:00
7:15
7:30
7:45
8:00
8:15
8:30
8:45
9:00
9:15
9:30
9:45
10:00
10:15
10:30
10:45

PACK MY BACKPACK

Are all items for school tomorrow in backpack? (✓)	

THURSDAY **DATE:** ____________ www.behaviorsciants.com

HOMEWORK FROM SCHOOL

Classes or Activities	Due Date	In Backpack? (✓)
Other Items to take home:		

FUTURE DUE DATES AND TESTS

THINGS TO WORK ON TODAY

MAKE A PLAN!

3:00
3:15
3:30
3:45
4:00
4:15
4:30
4:45
5:00
5:15
5:30
5:45
6:00
6:15
6:30
6:45
7:00
7:15
7:30
7:45
8:00
8:15
8:30
8:45
9:00
9:15
9:30
9:45
10:00
10:15
10:30
10:45

PACK MY BACKPACK

Are all items for school tomorrow in backpack? (✓)	

FRIDAY **DATE:** ____________________ www.behaviorsciants.com

HOMEWORK FROM SCHOOL

Classes or Activities	Due Date	In Backpack? (✓)
Other Items to take home:		

FUTURE DUE DATES AND TESTS

THINGS TO WORK ON TODAY

MAKE A PLAN!

3:00

3:15

3:30

3:45

4:00

4:15

4:30

4:45

5:00

5:15

5:30

5:45

6:00

6:15

6:30

6:45

7:00

7:15

7:30

7:45

8:00

8:15

8:30

8:45

9:00

9:15

9:30

9:45

10:00

10:15

10:30

10:45

PACK MY BACKPACK

Are all items for school tomorrow in backpack? (✓)	

SATURDAY DATE: ____________

MAKE A PLAN! 

9:00
9:30
10:00
10:30
11:00
11:30
12:00
12:30
1:00
1:30
2:00
2:30
3:00
3:30
4:00
4:30
5:00
5:30
6:00
6:30
7:00
7:30
8:00
8:30
9:00
9:30
10:00
10:30
11:00
11:30

THINGS TO WORK ON DURING THE WEEKEND 

SUNDAY DATE: ____________

MAKE A PLAN! 

9:00
9:30
10:00
10:30
11:00
11:30
12:00
12:30
1:00
1:30
2:00
2:30
3:00
3:30
4:00
4:30
5:00
5:30
6:00
6:30
7:00
7:30
8:00
8:30
9:00
9:30
10:00
10:30
11:00
11:30

PACK MY BACKPACK 

Are all items for school tomorrow in backpack? (✓)	

MONDAY **DATE:** ____________________ www.behaviorsciants.com

HOMEWORK FROM SCHOOL

Classes or Activities	Due Date	In Backpack? (✓)
Other Items to take home:		

FUTURE DUE DATES AND TESTS

THINGS TO WORK ON TODAY

MAKE A PLAN!

3:00
3:15
3:30
3:45
4:00
4:15
4:30
4:45
5:00
5:15
5:30
5:45
6:00
6:15
6:30
6:45
7:00
7:15
7:30
7:45
8:00
8:15
8:30
8:45
9:00
9:15
9:30
9:45
10:00
10:15
10:30
10:45

PACK MY BACKPACK

Are all items for school tomorrow in backpack? (✓)	

TUESDAY **DATE:** ____________________ www.behaviorsciants.com

HOMEWORK FROM SCHOOL

Classes or Activities	Due Date	In Backpack? (✓)
Other Items to take home:		

FUTURE DUE DATES AND TESTS

THINGS TO WORK ON TODAY

MAKE A PLAN!

3:00	
3:15	
3:30	
3:45	
4:00	
4:15	
4:30	
4:45	
5:00	
5:15	
5:30	
5:45	
6:00	
6:15	
6:30	
6:45	
7:00	
7:15	
7:30	
7:45	
8:00	
8:15	
8:30	
8:45	
9:00	
9:15	
9:30	
9:45	
10:00	
10:15	
10:30	
10:45	

PACK MY BACKPACK

Are all items for school tomorrow in backpack? (✓)	

WEDNESDAY **DATE:** ____________________ www.behaviorsciants.com

HOMEWORK FROM SCHOOL

Classes or Activities	Due Date	In Backpack? (✓)
Other Items to take home:		

FUTURE DUE DATES AND TESTS

THINGS TO WORK ON TODAY

MAKE A PLAN!

3:00	
3:15	
3:30	
3:45	
4:00	
4:15	
4:30	
4:45	
5:00	
5:15	
5:30	
5:45	
6:00	
6:15	
6:30	
6:45	
7:00	
7:15	
7:30	
7:45	
8:00	
8:15	
8:30	
8:45	
9:00	
9:15	
9:30	
9:45	
10:00	
10:15	
10:30	
10:45	

PACK MY BACKPACK

Are all items for school tomorrow in backpack? (✓)	

THURSDAY **DATE:** ____________________ www.behaviorsciants.com

HOMEWORK FROM SCHOOL 

Classes or Activities	Due Date	In Backpack? (✓)
Other Items to take home:		

FUTURE DUE DATES AND TESTS 

THINGS TO WORK ON TODAY  

MAKE A PLAN! 

3:00
3:15
3:30
3:45
4:00
4:15
4:30
4:45
5:00
5:15
5:30
5:45
6:00
6:15
6:30
6:45
7:00
7:15
7:30
7:45
8:00
8:15
8:30
8:45
9:00
9:15
9:30
9:45
10:00
10:15
10:30
10:45

PACK MY BACKPACK 

Are all items for school tomorrow in backpack? (✓)	

FRIDAY **DATE:** ____________________ www.behaviorsciants.com

HOMEWORK FROM SCHOOL

Classes or Activities	Due Date	In Backpack? (✓)
Other Items to take home:		

FUTURE DUE DATES AND TESTS

THINGS TO WORK ON TODAY

MAKE A PLAN!

3:00
3:15
3:30
3:45
4:00
4:15
4:30
4:45
5:00
5:15
5:30
5:45
6:00
6:15
6:30
6:45
7:00
7:15
7:30
7:45
8:00
8:15
8:30
8:45
9:00
9:15
9:30
9:45
10:00
10:15
10:30
10:45

PACK MY BACKPACK

Are all items for school tomorrow in backpack? (✓)	

SATURDAY DATE: ________

MAKE A PLAN! 

9:00	
9:30	
10:00	
10:30	
11:00	
11:30	
12:00	
12:30	
1:00	
1:30	
2:00	
2:30	
3:00	
3:30	
4:00	
4:30	
5:00	
5:30	
6:00	
6:30	
7:00	
7:30	
8:00	
8:30	
9:00	
9:30	
10:00	
10:30	
11:00	
11:30	

THINGS TO WORK ON DURING THE WEEKEND 

SUNDAY DATE: ________

MAKE A PLAN! 

9:00	
9:30	
10:00	
10:30	
11:00	
11:30	
12:00	
12:30	
1:00	
1:30	
2:00	
2:30	
3:00	
3:30	
4:00	
4:30	
5:00	
5:30	
6:00	
6:30	
7:00	
7:30	
8:00	
8:30	
9:00	
9:30	
10:00	
10:30	
11:00	
11:30	

PACK MY BACKPACK 

Are all items for school tomorrow in backpack? (✓)	

MONDAY **DATE:** ____________________ www.behaviorsciants.com

HOMEWORK FROM SCHOOL

Classes or Activities	Due Date	In Backpack? (✓)
Other Items to take home:		

FUTURE DUE DATES AND TESTS

THINGS TO WORK ON TODAY

MAKE A PLAN!

3:00	
3:15	
3:30	
3:45	
4:00	
4:15	
4:30	
4:45	
5:00	
5:15	
5:30	
5:45	
6:00	
6:15	
6:30	
6:45	
7:00	
7:15	
7:30	
7:45	
8:00	
8:15	
8:30	
8:45	
9:00	
9:15	
9:30	
9:45	
10:00	
10:15	
10:30	
10:45	

PACK MY BACKPACK

Are all items for school tomorrow in backpack? (✓)	

TUESDAY **DATE:** ____________________

www.behaviorsciants.com

HOMEWORK FROM SCHOOL 

Classes or Activities	Due Date	In Backpack? (✓)
Other Items to take home:		

FUTURE DUE DATES AND TESTS 

THINGS TO WORK ON TODAY 

MAKE A PLAN! 

3:00	
3:15	
3:30	
3:45	
4:00	
4:15	
4:30	
4:45	
5:00	
5:15	
5:30	
5:45	
6:00	
6:15	
6:30	
6:45	
7:00	
7:15	
7:30	
7:45	
8:00	
8:15	
8:30	
8:45	
9:00	
9:15	
9:30	
9:45	
10:00	
10:15	
10:30	
10:45	

PACK MY BACKPACK 

Are all items for school tomorrow in backpack? (✓)	

WEDNESDAY **DATE:** ____________________ www.behaviorsciants.com

HOMEWORK FROM SCHOOL

Classes or Activities	Due Date	In Backpack? (✓)
Other Items to take home:		

FUTURE DUE DATES AND TESTS

THINGS TO WORK ON TODAY

MAKE A PLAN!

3:00
3:15
3:30
3:45
4:00
4:15
4:30
4:45
5:00
5:15
5:30
5:45
6:00
6:15
6:30
6:45
7:00
7:15
7:30
7:45
8:00
8:15
8:30
8:45
9:00
9:15
9:30
9:45
10:00
10:15
10:30
10:45

PACK MY BACKPACK

Are all items for school tomorrow in backpack? (✓)	

THURSDAY **DATE:** ____________________

HOMEWORK FROM SCHOOL 

Classes or Activities	Due Date	In Backpack? (✓)
Other Items to take home:		

FUTURE DUE DATES AND TESTS 

THINGS TO WORK ON TODAY  

MAKE A PLAN!

3:00
3:15
3:30
3:45
4:00
4:15
4:30
4:45
5:00
5:15
5:30
5:45
6:00
6:15
6:30
6:45
7:00
7:15
7:30
7:45
8:00
8:15
8:30
8:45
9:00
9:15
9:30
9:45
10:00
10:15
10:30
10:45

PACK MY BACKPACK 

Are all items for school tomorrow in backpack? (✓)	

FRIDAY **DATE:** ____________________ www.behaviorsciants.com

HOMEWORK FROM SCHOOL 

Classes or Activities	Due Date	In Backpack? (✓)
Other Items to take home:		

FUTURE DUE DATES AND TESTS 

THINGS TO WORK ON TODAY 

MAKE A PLAN!

3:00
3:15
3:30
3:45
4:00
4:15
4:30
4:45
5:00
5:15
5:30
5:45
6:00
6:15
6:30
6:45
7:00
7:15
7:30
7:45
8:00
8:15
8:30
8:45
9:00
9:15
9:30
9:45
10:00
10:15
10:30
10:45

PACK MY BACKPACK 

Are all items for school tomorrow in backpack? (✓)	

SATURDAY **DATE:** ____________

MAKE A PLAN!

9:00
9:30
10:00
10:30
11:00
11:30
12:00
12:30
1:00
1:30
2:00
2:30
3:00
3:30
4:00
4:30
5:00
5:30
6:00
6:30
7:00
7:30
8:00
8:30
9:00
9:30
10:00
10:30
11:00
11:30

THINGS TO WORK ON DURING THE WEEKEND

SUNDAY **DATE:** ____________

MAKE A PLAN!

9:00
9:30
10:00
10:30
11:00
11:30
12:00
12:30
1:00
1:30
2:00
2:30
3:00
3:30
4:00
4:30
5:00
5:30
6:00
6:30
7:00
7:30
8:00
8:30
9:00
9:30
10:00
10:30
11:00
11:30

PACK MY BACKPACK

Are all items for school tomorrow in backpack? (✓)	

MONDAY **DATE:** ____________________ www.behaviorsciants.com

HOMEWORK FROM SCHOOL 

Classes or Activities	Due Date	In Backpack? (✓)
Other Items to take home:		

FUTURE DUE DATES AND TESTS 

THINGS TO WORK ON TODAY 

MAKE A PLAN! 

3:00
3:15
3:30
3:45
4:00
4:15
4:30
4:45
5:00
5:15
5:30
5:45
6:00
6:15
6:30
6:45
7:00
7:15
7:30
7:45
8:00
8:15
8:30
8:45
9:00
9:15
9:30
9:45
10:00
10:15
10:30
10:45

PACK MY BACKPACK 

Are all items for school tomorrow in backpack? (✓)	

TUESDAY **DATE:** ____________________

HOMEWORK FROM SCHOOL 

Classes or Activities	Due Date	In Backpack? (✓)
Other Items to take home:		

FUTURE DUE DATES AND TESTS 

THINGS TO WORK ON TODAY  

MAKE A PLAN!

3:00	
3:15	
3:30	
3:45	
4:00	
4:15	
4:30	
4:45	
5:00	
5:15	
5:30	
5:45	
6:00	
6:15	
6:30	
6:45	
7:00	
7:15	
7:30	
7:45	
8:00	
8:15	
8:30	
8:45	
9:00	
9:15	
9:30	
9:45	
10:00	
10:15	
10:30	
10:45	

PACK MY BACKPACK 

Are all items for school tomorrow in backpack? (✓)	

WEDNESDAY **DATE:** ____________________ www.behaviorsciants.com

HOMEWORK FROM SCHOOL 

Classes or Activities	Due Date	In Backpack? (✓)
Other Items to take home:		

FUTURE DUE DATES AND TESTS 

THINGS TO WORK ON TODAY 

MAKE A PLAN! 

3:00
3:15
3:30
3:45
4:00
4:15
4:30
4:45
5:00
5:15
5:30
5:45
6:00
6:15
6:30
6:45
7:00
7:15
7:30
7:45
8:00
8:15
8:30
8:45
9:00
9:15
9:30
9:45
10:00
10:15
10:30
10:45

PACK MY BACKPACK 

Are all items for school tomorrow in backpack? (✓)	

THURSDAY **DATE:** ____________________

HOMEWORK FROM SCHOOL

Classes or Activities	Due Date	In Backpack? (✓)
Other Items to take home:		

FUTURE DUE DATES AND TESTS

THINGS TO WORK ON TODAY

MAKE A PLAN!

3:00
3:15
3:30
3:45
4:00
4:15
4:30
4:45
5:00
5:15
5:30
5:45
6:00
6:15
6:30
6:45
7:00
7:15
7:30
7:45
8:00
8:15
8:30
8:45
9:00
9:15
9:30
9:45
10:00
10:15
10:30
10:45

PACK MY BACKPACK

Are all items for school tomorrow in backpack? (✓)	

FRIDAY **DATE:** ____________ www.behaviorsciants.com

HOMEWORK FROM SCHOOL 

Classes or Activities	Due Date	In Backpack? (✓)
Other Items to take home:		

FUTURE DUE DATES AND TESTS 

THINGS TO WORK ON TODAY 

MAKE A PLAN! 

3:00
3:15
3:30
3:45
4:00
4:15
4:30
4:45
5:00
5:15
5:30
5:45
6:00
6:15
6:30
6:45
7:00
7:15
7:30
7:45
8:00
8:15
8:30
8:45
9:00
9:15
9:30
9:45
10:00
10:15
10:30
10:45

PACK MY BACKPACK 

Are all items for school tomorrow in backpack? (✓)	

SATURDAY **DATE:** ____________

MAKE A PLAN!

9:00
9:30
10:00
10:30
11:00
11:30
12:00
12:30
1:00
1:30
2:00
2:30
3:00
3:30
4:00
4:30
5:00
5:30
6:00
6:30
7:00
7:30
8:00
8:30
9:00
9:30
10:00
10:30
11:00
11:30

THINGS TO WORK ON DURING THE WEEKEND

SUNDAY **DATE:** ____________

MAKE A PLAN!

9:00
9:30
10:00
10:30
11:00
11:30
12:00
12:30
1:00
1:30
2:00
2:30
3:00
3:30
4:00
4:30
5:00
5:30
6:00
6:30
7:00
7:30
8:00
8:30
9:00
9:30
10:00
10:30
11:00
11:30

PACK MY BACKPACK

Are all items for school tomorrow in backpack? (✓)	

References

Munoz, N. M., Pascual, A. C., & Robres, A. Q. (2019). The Relationship Between Executive Functions and Academic Performance in Primary Education: Review and Meta-Analysis. Frontiers in Psychology, 10, 1582–1582. https://doi.org/10.3389/fpsyg.2019.01582

Sesma, H. W., Mahone, E. M., Levine, T., Eason, S. H., & Cutting, L. E.(2009). The Contribution of Executive Skills to Reading Comprehension. Child Neuropsychology, 15(3), 232–246. https://doi.org/10.1080/09297040802220029

Zelazo, P. D., & Carlson, S. M. (2012). Hot and Cool Executive Function in Childhood and Adolescence: Development and Plasticity. Child Development Perspectives, 6(4), 354–360. https://doi.org/10.1111/j.1750-8606.2012.00246.x

About the Author

Stephanie Chan, Ph.D.c., M.Ed., is a researcher, bestselling author, early childhood educator, and Board-Certified Behavior Analyst (BCBA). With extensive training in early childhood education, psychology, and behavior analysis, and many years of experience working with young children, Stephanie was one of the first to uniquely apply behavior science to children's literature. She has published many children's books and educational materials, primarily focusing on perspective-taking, problem-solving, developing and maintaining friendships, understanding and regulating emotions and feelings, and Acceptance and Commitment Therapy (ACT), all grounded on contextual behavioral science. In addition, she published scientific papers in top-tier journals and presented her research findings at international conferences covering various topics.

Stephanie is also the clinical director of the non-profit organization PlaySmart Child Development Society and the editor-in-chief of the publisher Behavior SciAnts. She regularly organizes training workshops for parents and practitioners worldwide to help children improve social skills and behavior issues. Readers who purchase books in any of the series can receive ongoing training and behavior support and become a member of the community.

Made in the USA
Columbia, SC
13 May 2024

35613226R00098